MW01279959

DRAW NEAR TO GOD

2014

PRAYER JOURNAL

Published by The Word Among Us Press
7115 Guilford Drive, Suite 100
Frederick, Maryland 21704
www.wau.org

ISBN: 978-1-59325-226-7

Compiled by Jeanne Kun

Cover design by John Hamilton Designs

Front cover: Tetons, Thinkstock Photos

Printed in China

Dear Friend in Christ,

"Draw near to God, and he will draw near to you." With this compelling invitation from the Letter of James (4:8), we are encouraged to come into the Lord's presence, assured that he delights in being with us. In fact, as much as we seek to draw near to God, even more does he long to draw near to us.

Thus, it is fitting that the theme for this year's *Prayer Journal* is taken from this Scripture verse. What better way to come closer to God than through daily prayer! When we take time each day to praise and thank the Lord, call upon him for his help and mercy, and reflect on his word in Scripture, we find that we are on a pathway that leads us straight to him.

Each day we can encounter the Lord in our time of prayer and Scripture reading. There we draw near to him, offering him our love and praise and opening our hearts to him. There we can tell him of our cares, asking his forgiveness for our sins and his healing for our wounds and ills. There we can share with him our plans and dreams, seeking his guidance for the decisions we face on the pathway through life. And there God will draw near to us, revealing his heart of mercy to us, comforting and strengthening us with his love, instructing us with his truth, and transforming our lives through the power of his Spirit.

As in the past, this year's *Prayer Journal* provides the Mass readings for each day of the year. In 2014 the Church is following Cycle A, with the Gospel readings for the Sundays in Ordinary Time taken from the Gospel of Matthew. At the top of each page of the journal, you will find a short Scripture verse or quotation from a saint, an ancient or contemporary Christian writer, or a Church document. Many of these texts reflect the journal's theme, "Draw Near to God," while others correspond to the feast days of the saints, special holy days and seasons in the liturgical year, or the Scripture readings from the Mass of the day.

In addition, at the beginning of each month, there is a longer, inspirational quote. You may want to reflect on the monthly selection and keep it in mind throughout the following four weeks so that your desire to stay close to the Lord will continue to grow.

One of the primary benefits of keeping a prayer journal is to record—and later recall—the insights and impulses that are meaningful to us in our encounters with the Lord. "I advise you strongly," St. Francis Xavier wrote, "to make a little journal, and to note down carefully in it the secret illuminations with which God has enlightened your mind in your daily meditations." He explained:

> I earnestly advise you to write down, as a help to your memory, those heavenly lights which our merciful God often gives to the soul which draws near to him, and with which he will also enlighten yours when you strive to know his will in meditation, for they are more deeply impressed on the mind by the very act and occupation of writing them down. And should it happen, as it usually does, that in the course of time these things are either less vividly remembered or entirely forgotten, they will come with fresh life to the mind reading them over.

Making note of a Scripture verse that particularly speaks to you; composing your own prayers that express your love, gratitude, and praise to the Lord; confiding to him your personal needs and struggles, your deepest longings and hopes—these are just a few more ways that you might use this journal. And at the end of the year, you'll have a convenient record that you can leaf through to recall how the Lord has worked in your life.

As we progress toward God day by day on the pathway of prayer, may we all find that he, too, delights in drawing near to us!

The Word Among Us Press

Abbreviations of
Books of the Bible

Acts Acts of the Apostles

Am Amos

Bar Baruch

1 Chr
1 Chronicles

2 Chr
2 Chronicles

Col Colossians

1 Cor
1 Corinthians

2 Cor
2 Corinthians

Dn Daniel

Dt Deuteronomy

Eccl Ecclesiastes

Eph Ephesians

Est Esther

Ex Exodus

Ez Ezekiel

Ezr Ezra

Gal Galatians

Gn Genesis

Hb Habakkuk

Heb Hebrews

Hg Haggai

Hos Hosea

Is Isaiah

Jas James

Jb Job

Jdt Judith

Jer Jeremiah

Jgs Judges

Jl Joel

Jn John

1 Jn 1 John

2 Jn 2 John

3 Jn 3 John

Jon Jonah

Jos Joshua

Jude Jude

1 Kgs 1 Kings

2 Kgs 2 Kings

Lam Lamentations

Lk Luke

Lv Leviticus

Mal Malachi

1 Mc 1 Maccabees

2 Mc 2 Maccabees

Mi Micah

Mk Mark

Mt Matthew

Na Nahum

Neh Nehemiah

Nm Numbers

Ob Obadiah

Phil Philippians

Phlm Philemon

Prv Proverbs

Ps Psalms

1 Pt 1 Peter

2 Pt 2 Peter

Rom Romans

Ru Ruth

Rv Revelation

Sg Song of Songs

Sir Sirach

1 Sm 1 Samuel

2 Sm 2 Samuel

Tb Tobit

1 Thes
1 Thessalonians

2 Thes
2 Thessalonians

Ti Titus

1 Tm 1 Timothy

2 Tm 2 Timothy

Wis Wisdom

Zec Zechariah

Zep Zephaniah

January 2014

S	M	T	W	T	F	S
			1	2	3	4
5	6	7	8	9	10	11
12	13	14	15	16	17	18
19	20	21	22	23	24	25
26	27	28	29	30	31	

February 2014

S	M	T	W	T	F	S
						1
2	3	4	5	6	7	8
9	10	11	12	13	14	15
16	17	18	19	20	21	22
23	24	25	26	27	28	

March 2014

S	M	T	W	T	F	S
						1
2	3	4	5	6	7	8
9	10	11	12	13	14	15
16	17	18	19	20	21	22
23	24	25	26	27	28	29
30	31					

April 2014

S	M	T	W	T	F	S
		1	2	3	4	5
6	7	8	9	10	11	12
13	14	15	16	17	18	19
20	21	22	23	24	25	26
27	28	29	30			

May 2014

S	M	T	W	T	F	S
				1	2	3
4	5	6	7	8	9	10
11	12	13	14	15	16	17
18	19	20	21	22	23	24
25	26	27	28	29	30	31

June 2014

S	M	T	W	T	F	S
1	2	3	4	5	6	7
8	9	10	11	12	13	14
15	16	17	18	19	20	21
22	23	24	25	26	27	28
29	30					

July 2014

S	M	T	W	T	F	S
		1	2	3	4	5
6	7	8	9	10	11	12
13	14	15	16	17	18	19
20	21	22	23	24	25	26
27	28	29	30	31		

August 2014

S	M	T	W	T	F	S
					1	2
3	4	5	6	7	8	9
10	11	12	13	14	15	16
17	18	19	20	21	22	23
24	25	26	27	28	29	30
31						

September 2014

S	M	T	W	T	F	S
	1	2	3	4	5	6
7	8	9	10	11	12	13
14	15	16	17	18	19	20
21	22	23	24	25	26	27
28	29	30				

October 2014

S	M	T	W	T	F	S
			1	2	3	4
5	6	7	8	9	10	11
12	13	14	15	16	17	18
19	20	21	22	23	24	25
26	27	28	29	30	31	

November 2014

S	M	T	W	T	F	S
						1
2	3	4	5	6	7	8
9	10	11	12	13	14	15
16	17	18	19	20	21	22
23	24	25	26	27	28	29
30						

December 2014

S	M	T	W	T	F	S
	1	2	3	4	5	6
7	8	9	10	11	12	13
14	15	16	17	18	19	20
21	22	23	24	25	26	27
28	29	30	31			

January 2015

S	M	T	W	T	F	S
				1	2	3
4	5	6	7	8	9	10
11	12	13	14	15	16	17
18	19	20	21	22	23	24
25	26	27	28	29	30	31

May 2015

S	M	T	W	T	F	S
					1	2
3	4	5	6	7	8	9
10	11	12	13	14	15	16
17	18	19	20	21	22	23
24	25	26	27	28	29	30
31						

September 2015

S	M	T	W	T	F	S
		1	2	3	4	5
6	7	8	9	10	11	12
13	14	15	16	17	18	19
20	21	22	23	24	25	26
27	28	29	30			

February 2015

S	M	T	W	T	F	S
1	2	3	4	5	6	7
8	9	10	11	12	13	14
15	16	17	18	19	20	21
22	23	24	25	26	27	28

June 2015

S	M	T	W	T	F	S
	1	2	3	4	5	6
7	8	9	10	11	12	13
14	15	16	17	18	19	20
21	22	23	24	25	26	27
28	29	30				

October 2015

S	M	T	W	T	F	S
				1	2	3
4	5	6	7	8	9	10
11	12	13	14	15	16	17
18	19	20	21	22	23	24
25	26	27	28	29	30	31

March 2015

S	M	T	W	T	F	S
1	2	3	4	5	6	7
8	9	10	11	12	13	14
15	16	17	18	19	20	21
22	23	24	25	26	27	28
29	30	31				

July 2015

S	M	T	W	T	F	S
			1	2	3	4
5	6	7	8	9	10	11
12	13	14	15	16	17	18
19	20	21	22	23	24	25
26	27	28	29	30	31	

November 2015

S	M	T	W	T	F	S
1	2	3	4	5	6	7
8	9	10	11	12	13	14
15	16	17	18	19	20	21
22	23	24	25	26	27	28
29	30					

April 2015

S	M	T	W	T	F	S
			1	2	3	4
5	6	7	8	9	10	11
12	13	14	15	16	17	18
19	20	21	22	23	24	25
26	27	28	29	30		

August 2015

S	M	T	W	T	F	S
						1
2	3	4	5	6	7	8
9	10	11	12	13	14	15
16	17	18	19	20	21	22
23	24	25	26	27	28	29
30	31					

December 2015

S	M	T	W	T	F	S
		1	2	3	4	5
6	7	8	9	10	11	12
13	14	15	16	17	18	19
20	21	22	23	24	25	26
27	28	29	30	31		

JANUARY

Cast away your troublesome cares, put aside your wearisome distractions. Give yourself a little leisure to converse with God, and take your rest awhile in him. Enter into the secret chamber of your heart; leave everything outside but God . . . and when you have shut the door, then truly seek him.

—*St. Anselm*

Virgin Mary, hear my prayer: Through the Holy Spirit
you became the mother of Jesus;
from the Holy Spirit may I, too, have Jesus.

—St. Ildephonsus

1 Wednesday

SOLEMNITY OF MARY, THE HOLY MOTHER OF GOD
• Nm 6:22-27 • Ps 67:2-3, 5-6, 8 • Gal 4:4-7 • Lk 2:16-21
Holy Day of Obligation

_____

_____

_____

_____

_____

_____

_____

_____

2 Thursday

SAINTS BASIL THE GREAT AND GREGORY NAZIANZEN
• 1 Jn 2:22-28 • Ps 98:1-4 • Jn 1:19-28

_____

_____

_____

_____

_____

_____

_____

_____

> To pray "Jesus" is to invoke him and to call him within us. His name is the only one that contains the presence it signifies.
>
> —*Catechism of the Catholic Church,* **2666**

THE MOST HOLY NAME OF JESUS
• 1 Jn 2:29–3:6 • Ps 98:1, 3c-6 • Jn 1:29-34

3
Friday

_____

_____

_____

_____

_____

_____

_____

_____

_____

_____

SAINT ELIZABETH ANN SETON
• 1 Jn 3:7-10 • Ps 98:1, 7-9 • Jn 1:35-42

4
Saturday

_____

_____

_____

_____

_____

_____

_____

_____

_____

_____

JANUARY

The same Christ who in Bethlehem, as a Child, accepted the gifts of the Magi Kings is still the One to whom men and whole peoples "open their treasures."

—**Blessed John Paul II**

5
Sunday

THE EPIPHANY OF THE LORD
• Is 60:1-6 • Ps 72:1-2, 7-8, 10-13 • Eph 3:2-3a, 5-6 • Mt 2:1-12

_____

_____

_____

_____

_____

_____

_____

_____

6
Monday

SAINT ANDRÉ BESSETTE
• 1 Jn 3:22–4:6 • Ps 2:7bc-8, 10-12a • Mt 4:12-17, 23-25

_____

_____

_____

_____

_____

_____

_____

_____

May God shelter you from disturbance in the hidden recesses
of his love, until he brings you at last into that place of fullness
where you will repose forever in the vision of peace.

—St. Raymond of Penyafort

SAINT RAYMOND OF PENYAFORT
• 1 Jn 4:7-10 • Ps 72:1-4, 7-8 • Mk 6:34-44

7
Tuesday

_____

_____

_____

_____

_____

_____

_____

_____

_____

_____

• 1 Jn 4:11-18 • Ps 72:1-2, 10, 12-13 • Mk 6:45-52

8
Wednesday

_____

_____

_____

_____

_____

_____

_____

_____

_____

_____

JANUARY

We love because [God] first loved us.

—1 John 4:19

9
Thursday

• 1 Jn 4:19–5:4 • Ps 72:1-2, 14-15, 17 • Lk 4:14-22a

_____

_____

_____

_____

_____

_____

_____

_____

_____

10
Friday

• 1 Jn 5:5-13 • Ps 147:12-15, 19-20 • Lk 5:12-16

_____

_____

_____

_____

_____

_____

_____

_____

_____

_____

The Lord was baptized, not to be cleansed himself, but to cleanse the waters, so that those waters, cleansed by the flesh of Christ which knew no sin, might have the power of baptism.

—St. Ambrose

• 1 Jn 5:14-21 • Ps 149:1-6a, 9b • Jn 3:22-30

11
Saturday

THE BAPTISM OF THE LORD
• Is 42:1-4, 6-7 • Ps 29:1-4, 9-10 • Acts 10:34-38 • Mt 3:13-17

12
Sunday

JANUARY

O God, fill with wind the sails I have hoisted for you,
and carry me forward on my course.

—**St. Hilary**

13
Monday

SAINT HILARY
• 1 Sm 1:1-8 • Ps 116:12-19 • Mk 1:14-20

_____

_____

_____

_____

_____

_____

_____

_____

_____

14
Tuesday

• 1 Sm 1:9-20 • (Ps) 1 Sm 2:1, 4-8 • Mk 1:21-28

_____

_____

_____

_____

_____

_____

_____

_____

_____

You have multiplied, O LORD my God,
your wondrous deeds and your thoughts toward us;
none can compare with you.

—Psalm 40:5

• 1 Sm 3:1-10, 19-20 • Ps 40:2, 5, 7-10 • Mk 1:29-39

15
Wednesday

_____

_____

_____

_____

_____

_____

_____

_____

_____

_____

• 1 Sm 4:1-11 • Ps 44:10-11, 14-15, 24-25 • Mk 1:40-45

16
Thursday

_____

_____

_____

_____

_____

_____

_____

_____

_____

JANUARY

> If the soul surrenders itself to the Lord with all its might,
> the righteous God will grant it true repentance.
>
> —**St. Anthony**

17
Friday

SAINT ANTHONY
• 1 Sm 8:4-7, 10-22a • Ps 89:16-19 • Mk 2:1-12

_____
_____
_____
_____
_____
_____
_____
_____
_____

18
Saturday

• 1 Sm 9:1-4, 17-19; 10:1a • Ps 21:2-7 • Mk 2:13-17

_____
_____
_____
_____
_____
_____
_____
_____
_____

> Those who bring thanksgiving as their sacrifice honor me;
> to those who go the right way
> I will show the salvation of God.
>
> —Psalm 50:23

SECOND SUNDAY IN ORDINARY TIME
• Is 49:3, 5-6 • Ps 40:2, 4, 7-10 • 1 Cor 1:1-3 • Jn 1:29-34

19
Sunday

_____

_____

_____

_____

_____

_____

_____

_____

_____

_____

SAINT FABIAN; SAINT SEBASTIAN
• 1 Sm 15:16-23 • Ps 50:8-9, 16b-17, 21, 23 • Mk 2:18-22

20
Monday

_____

_____

_____

_____

_____

_____

_____

_____

_____

_____

JANUARY

Christ will guard his own.

—St. Agnes

21
Tuesday

SAINT AGNES
• 1 Sm 16:1-13 • Ps 89:20-22, 27-28 • Mk 2:23-28

_____
_____
_____
_____
_____
_____
_____
_____
_____

22
Wednesday

DAY OF PRAYER FOR THE LEGAL PROTECTION OF
UNBORN CHILDREN
• 1 Sm 17:32-33, 37, 40-51 • Ps 144:1b-2, 9-10 • Mk 3:1-6

_____
_____
_____
_____
_____
_____
_____
_____
_____

> O great and good Creator, how much do I owe to you, since out of my nothingness you have made me what I am!
>
> —St. Francis de Sales

SAINT VINCENT
• 1 Sm 18:6-9; 19:1-7 • Ps 56:2-3, 9-13 • Mk 3:7-12

23
Thursday

_____
_____
_____
_____
_____
_____
_____
_____
_____
_____

SAINT FRANCIS DE SALES
• 1 Sm 24:3-21 • Ps 57:2-4, 6, 11 • Mk 3:13-19

24
Friday

_____
_____
_____
_____
_____
_____
_____
_____
_____
_____

JANUARY

I am the least of the apostles, unfit to be called an apostle, because I persecuted the church of God. But by the grace of God I am what I am, and his grace towards me has not been in vain.

—St. Paul in 1 Corinthians 15:9-19

25 Saturday

THE CONVERSION OF SAINT PAUL THE APOSTLE
• Acts 22:3-16 or Acts 9:1-22 • Ps 117:1b-2 • Mk 16:15-18

_____

_____

_____

_____

_____

_____

_____

_____

26 Sunday

THIRD SUNDAY IN ORDINARY TIME
• Is 8:23–9:3 • Ps 27:1, 4, 13-14 • 1 Cor 1:10-13, 17 • Mt 4:12-23

_____

_____

_____

_____

_____

_____

_____

_____

_____

> In order to be an instrument in God's hands,
> we must be of no account in our own eyes.
>
> —**St. Angela Merici**

Saint Angela Merici
• 2 Sm 5:1-7, 10 • Ps 89:20-22, 25-26 • Mk 3:22-30

27
Monday

Saint Thomas Aquinas
• 2 Sm 6:12b-15, 17-19 • Ps 24:7-10 • Mk 3:31-35

28
Tuesday

JANUARY

Let the heavens proclaim your wonders, O LORD,
your faithfulness in the assembly of the holy ones.

—**Psalm 89:5**

29
Wednesday

• 2 Sm 7:4-17 • Ps 89:4-5, 27-30 • Mk 4:1-20

_____

_____

_____

_____

_____

_____

_____

_____

30
Thursday

• 2 Sm 7:18-19, 24-29 • Ps 132:1-5, 11-14 • Mk 4:21-25

_____

_____

_____

_____

_____

_____

_____

_____

_____

All for God and for his glory. In whatever you do,
think of the glory of God as your main goal.

—St. John Bosco

SAINT JOHN BOSCO
• 2 Sm 11:1-4a, 5-10a, 13-17 • Ps 51:3-7, 10-11 • Mk 4:26-34

31
Friday

_____
_____
_____
_____
_____
_____
_____
_____
_____
_____
_____
_____
_____
_____
_____
_____
_____
_____
_____
_____
_____
_____

JANUARY

FEBRUARY

Prayer and faith united are unimaginably powerful. . . . Always pray with Jesus, remembering that a person united with Jesus can do everything. Keep this verse in mind: "I can do all things in Christ who strengthens me" (Philippians 4:13). Have faith, pray with faith, and good and overflowing measure will be given you.

—*St. Frances Xavier Cabrini*

> The Presentation of Jesus in the Temple manifests the wisdom of Simeon and Anna, the wisdom of a life dedicated totally to the search for the face of God.
>
> **—Pope Benedict XVI**

1
Saturday
• 2 Sm 12:1-7a, 10-17 • Ps 51:12-17 • Mk 4:35-41

_____

_____

_____

_____

_____

_____

_____

_____

2
Sunday
THE PRESENTATION OF THE LORD
• Mal 3:1-4 • Ps 24:7-10 • Heb 2:14-18 • Lk 2:22-40

_____

_____

_____

_____

_____

_____

_____

_____

If I were worthy of such a favor from my God, I would ask that
he grant me this one miracle: that by his grace
he would make of me a good man.

—**St. Ansgar**

SAINT BLAISE; SAINT ANSGAR
• 2 Sm 15:13-14, 30; 16:5-13 • Ps 3:2-7 • Mk 5:1-20

3
Monday

_____

_____

_____

_____

_____

_____

_____

_____

_____

• 2 Sm 18:9-10, 14b, 24-25a, 30–19:3 • Ps 86:1-6 • Mk 5:21-43

4
Tuesday

_____

_____

_____

_____

_____

_____

_____

_____

_____

FEBRUARY

Jesus Christ, Lord of all, you see my heart, you know my desires.
You alone possess all that I am.

—**St. Agatha**

5
Wednesday

SAINT AGATHA
• 2 Sm 24:2, 9-17 • Ps 32:1-2, 5-7 • Mk 6:1-6

_____

_____

_____

_____

_____

_____

_____

6
Thursday

SAINT PAUL MIKI AND COMPANIONS
• 1 Kgs 2:1-4, 10-12 • (Ps) 1 Chr 29:10-12 • Mk 6:7-13

_____

_____

_____

_____

_____

_____

_____

_____

When a person loves another dearly, he desires strongly
to be close to the other: therefore, why be afraid to die?
Death brings us to God!

—St. Josephine Bakhita

• Sir 47:2-11 • Ps 18:31, 47, 50-51 • Mk 6:14-29

7
Friday

_____
_____
_____
_____
_____
_____
_____
_____
_____
_____

SAINT JEROME EMILIANI; SAINT JOSEPHINE BAKHITA
• 1 Kgs 3:4-13 • Ps 119:9-14 • Mk 6:30-34

8
Saturday

_____
_____
_____
_____
_____
_____
_____
_____
_____
_____

FEBRUARY

Let your light shine before others, so that they may see your good works and give glory to your Father in heaven.

—**Jesus in Matthew 5:16**

9
Sunday

FIFTH SUNDAY IN ORDINARY TIME
• Is 58:7-10 • Ps 112:4-9 • 1 Cor 2:1-5 • Mt 5:13-16

_____
_____
_____
_____
_____
_____
_____
_____
_____

10
Monday

SAINT SCHOLASTICA
• 1 Kgs 8:1-7, 9-13 • Ps 132:6-10 • Mk 6:53-56

_____
_____
_____
_____
_____
_____
_____
_____
_____

Grant, most tender of mothers, that I may be a child after your
own heart and that of your divine Son.

—**St. Bernadette Soubirous**

OUR LADY OF LOURDES
• 1 Kgs 8:22-23, 27-30 • Ps 84:3-5, 10-11 • Mk 7:1-13

11
Tuesday

_____

_____

_____

_____

_____

_____

_____

_____

_____

_____

• 1 Kgs 10:1-10 • Ps 37:5-6, 30-31, 39-40 • Mk 7:14-23

12
Wednesday

_____

_____

_____

_____

_____

_____

_____

_____

_____

_____

FEBRUARY

O Lord my God, build up your church and gather all into unity.
—St. Cyril

13
Thursday
• 1 Kgs 11:4-13 • Ps 106:3-4, 35-37, 40 • Mk 7:24-30

_____

_____

_____

_____

_____

_____

_____

_____

_____

14
Friday
SAINTS CYRIL AND METHODIUS
• 1 Kgs 11:29-32; 12:19 • Ps 81:10-15 • Mk 7:31-37

_____

_____

_____

_____

_____

_____

_____

_____

_____

When I am incapable of praying, I want to keep telling him that I love him. It's not difficult, and it keeps the fire going.

—**St. Thérèse of Lisieux**

• 1 Kgs 12:26-32; 13:33-34 • Ps 106:6-7b, 19-22 • Mk 8:1-10

15
Saturday

_____

_____

_____

_____

_____

_____

_____

_____

_____

SIXTH SUNDAY IN ORDINARY TIME
• Sir 15:15-20 • Ps 119:1-2, 4-5, 17-18, 33-34 • 1 Cor 2:6-10
• Mt 5:17-37

16
Sunday

_____

_____

_____

_____

_____

_____

_____

_____

_____

_____

FEBRUARY

When the cares of my heart are many,
your consolations cheer my soul.

—Psalm 94:19

17
Monday

THE SEVEN HOLY FOUNDERS OF THE SERVITE ORDER
• Jas 1:1-11 • Ps 119:67-68, 71-72, 75-76 • Mk 8:11-13

_____

_____

_____

_____

_____

_____

_____

_____

18
Tuesday

• Jas 1:12-18 • Ps 94:12-15, 18-19 • Mk 8:14-21

_____

_____

_____

_____

_____

_____

_____

_____

_____

Prayer . . . vanquishes all the strength of the tempter,
and it changes men from blind into seeing, from weak into
strong, from sinners into saints.

—St. Alphonsus Liguori

• Jas 1:19-27 • Ps 15:2-5 • Mk 8:22-26

19
Wednesday

_____

_____

_____

_____

_____

_____

_____

_____

_____

• Jas 2:1-9 • Ps 34:2-7 • Mk 8:27-33

20
Thursday

_____

_____

_____

_____

_____

_____

_____

_____

_____

_____

FEBRUARY

Let Christ always abide in your heart by the fire of his love.

—St. Peter Damian

21
Friday

SAINT PETER DAMIAN
• Jas 2:14-24, 26 • Ps 112:1-6 • Mk 8:34–9:1

_____
_____
_____
_____
_____
_____
_____
_____
_____

22
Saturday

THE CHAIR OF SAINT PETER THE APOSTLE
• 1 Pt 5:1-4 • Ps 23:1-6 • Mt 16:13-19

_____
_____
_____
_____
_____
_____
_____
_____
_____

Bless the LORD, O my soul,
and all that is within me,
bless his holy name.

—**Psalm 103:1**

SEVENTH SUNDAY IN ORDINARY TIME
• Lev 19:1-2, 17-18 • Ps 103:1-4, 8, 10, 12-13 • 1 Cor 3:16-23
• Mt 5:38-48

23
Sunday

_____

_____

_____

_____

_____

_____

_____

_____

_____

• Jas 3:13-18 • Ps 19:8-10, 15 • Mk 9:14-29

24
Monday

_____

_____

_____

_____

_____

_____

_____

_____

_____

FEBRUARY

You don't need to use many or high-sounding words. Just repeat often, "Lord, show me your mercy as you know best."
Or, "God, come to my assistance."

—**St. Macarius of Alexandria**

25
Tuesday

• Jas 4:1-10 • Ps 55:7-11a, 23 • Mk 9:30-37

_____
_____
_____
_____
_____
_____
_____
_____
_____

26
Wednesday

• Jas 4:13-17 • Ps 49:2-3, 6-11 • Mk 9:38-40

_____
_____
_____
_____
_____
_____
_____
_____
_____

The time we spend in having our daily audience with God is the most precious part of the whole day.

—Blessed Teresa of Calcutta

• Jas 5:1-6 • Ps 49:14-20 • Mk 9:41-50

27
Thursday

_____
_____
_____
_____
_____
_____
_____
_____
_____

• Jas 5:9-12 • Ps 103:1-4, 8-9, 11-12 • Mk 10:1-12

28
Friday

_____
_____
_____
_____
_____
_____
_____
_____
_____
_____

FEBRUARY

MARCH

M y Lord and my God,
take me from all that keeps me from you.
My Lord and my God,
grant me all that leads me to you.
My Lord and my God,
take me from myself and give me
    completely to you.

—*St. Nicholas of Flue*

The Lord is good to the soul that seeks him. Seek him by your
prayers, seek him by your actions, find him by your faith.
—**St. Bernard of Clairvaux**

1
Saturday

• Jas 5:13-20 • Ps 141:1-3, 8 • Mk 10:13-16

_____

_____

_____

_____

_____

_____

_____

_____

2
Sunday

EIGHTH SUNDAY IN ORDINARY TIME
• Is 49:14-15 • Ps 62:2-3, 6-9 • 1 Cor 4:1-5 • Mt 6:24-34

_____

_____

_____

_____

_____

_____

_____

_____

Love! Love! Let us give ourselves to real pure love.
                                    —St. Katharine Drexel

SAINT KATHARINE DREXEL
• 1 Pt 1:3-9 • Ps 111:1-2, 5-6, 9-10 • Mk 10:17-27

3
Monday

_____

_____

_____

_____

_____

_____

_____

_____

_____

_____

SAINT CASIMIR
• 1 Pt 1:10-16 • Ps 98:1-4 • Mk 10:28-31

4
Tuesday

_____

_____

_____

_____

_____

_____

_____

_____

_____

MARCH

During Lent let us improve our spirit of prayer and recollection. Let us free our minds from all that is not Jesus.

—**Blessed Teresa of Calcutta**

5
Wednesday

ASH WEDNESDAY
• Jl 2:12-18 • Ps 51:3-6b, 12-14, 17 • 2 Cor 5:20–6:2 • Mt 6:1-6, 16-18

_____

_____

_____

_____

_____

_____

_____

_____

_____

6
Thursday

• Dt 30:15-20 • Ps 1:1-4, 6 • Lk 9:22-25

_____

_____

_____

_____

_____

_____

_____

_____

_____

When you feel depressed, reflect on the passion of
Our Lord Jesus Christ and his precious wounds,
and you will experience great consolation.

—St. John of God

SAINTS PERPETUA AND FELICITY
• Is 58:1-9a • Ps 51:3-6b, 18-19 • Mt 9:14-15

7
Friday

_____

_____

_____

_____

_____

_____

_____

_____

_____

SAINT JOHN OF GOD
• Is 58:9b-14 • Ps 86:1-6 • Lk 5:27-32

8
Saturday

_____

_____

_____

_____

_____

_____

_____

_____

_____

MARCH

The sacrifice acceptable to God is a broken spirit;
a broken and contrite heart, O God, you will not despise.

—Psalm 51:17

9
Sunday

FIRST SUNDAY OF LENT
• Gn 2:7-9; 3:1-7 • Ps 51:3-6, 12-13, 17 • Rom 5:12-19 • Mt 4:1-11

_____

_____

_____

_____

_____

_____

_____

_____

_____

10
Monday

• Lv 19:1-2, 11-18 • Ps 19:8-10, 15 • Mt 25:31-46

_____

_____

_____

_____

_____

_____

_____

_____

_____

Lord, give us life, make us live from you as our source,
and grant that we, too, may be sources, wellsprings capable of
bestowing the water of life in our time.

—**Pope Benedict XVI**

• Is 55:10-11 • Ps 34:4-7, 16-19 • Mt 6:7-15

11
Tuesday

_____

_____

_____

_____

_____

_____

_____

_____

_____

_____

• Jon 3:1-10 • Ps 51:3-4, 12-13, 18-19 • Lk 11:29-32

12
Wednesday

_____

_____

_____

_____

_____

_____

_____

_____

_____

_____

MARCH

The LORD will fulfill his purpose for me;
your steadfast love, O LORD, endures forever.
Do not forsake the work of your hands.

—**Psalm 138:8**

13
Thursday

• Est C:12, 14-16, 23-25 • Ps 138:1-3, 7c-8 • Mt 7:7-12

_____

_____

_____

_____

_____

_____

_____

_____

_____

14
Friday

• Ez 18:21-28 • Ps 130:1-8 • Mt 5:20-26

_____

_____

_____

_____

_____

_____

_____

_____

_____

How good it is to trust God! Turn to him often, as children look to their father and mother in their needs.

—**St. Louise de Marillac**

• Dt 26:16-19 • Ps 119:1-2, 4-5, 7-8 • Mt 5:43-48

15
Saturday

_____
_____
_____
_____
_____
_____
_____
_____
_____
_____

SECOND SUNDAY OF LENT
• Gn 12:1-4a • Ps 33:4-5, 18-20, 22 • 2 Tm 1:8b-10 • Mt 17:1-9

16
Sunday

_____
_____
_____
_____
_____
_____
_____
_____
_____

MARCH

Christ with me, Christ before me, Christ behind me,
Christ within me, Christ beneath me, Christ above me,
Christ at my right, Christ at my left.

—**St. Patrick's Breastplate**

17
Monday

SAINT PATRICK
• Dn 9:4b-10 • Ps 79:8-9, 11, 13 • Lk 6:36-38

_____

_____

_____

_____

_____

_____

_____

_____

_____

18
Tuesday

SAINT CYRIL OF JERUSALEM
• Is 1:10, 16-20 • Ps 50:8-9, 16b-17, 21, 23 • Mt 23:1-12

_____

_____

_____

_____

_____

_____

_____

_____

_____

Anyone who cannot find a master to teach him prayer
should take this glorious saint [Joseph] for his master,
and he will not go astray.

—St. Teresa of Avila

SAINT JOSEPH, SPOUSE OF THE BLESSED VIRGIN MARY
• 2 Sm 7:4-5a, 12-14a, 16 • Ps 89:2-5, 27, 29 • Rom 4:13, 16-18, 22
• Mt 1:16, 18-21, 24a or Lk 2:41-51a

19
Wednesday

_____

_____

_____

_____

_____

_____

_____

_____

_____

• Jer 17:5-10 • Ps 1:1-4, 6 • Lk 16:19-31

20
Thursday

_____

_____

_____

_____

_____

_____

_____

_____

_____

MARCH

He will again have compassion upon us;
he will tread our iniquities underfoot.

—Micah 7:19

21
Friday

• Gn 37:3-4, 12-13a, 17b-28a • Ps 105:16-21 • Mt 21:33-43, 45-46

_____

_____

_____

_____

_____

_____

_____

_____

_____

22
Saturday

• Mi 7:14-15, 18-20 • Ps 103:1-4, 9-12 • Lk 15:1-3, 11-32

_____

_____

_____

_____

_____

_____

_____

_____

_____

O come, let us sing to the LORD;
let us make a joyful noise to the rock of our salvation!

—**Psalm 95:1**

THIRD SUNDAY OF LENT
• Ex 17:3-7 • Ps 95:1-2, 6-9 • Rom 5:1-2, 5-8 • Jn 4:5-42

23
Sunday

_____

_____

_____

_____

_____

_____

_____

_____

_____

_____

• 2 Kgs 5:1-15b • Ps 42:2-3; 43:3-4 • Lk 4:24-30

24
Monday

_____

_____

_____

_____

_____

_____

_____

_____

_____

MARCH

Ask Mary to lead you to Jesus and you will know
what it is to live by his side.
—**Cardinal Francis Xavier Nguyen Van Thuan**

25
Tuesday

THE ANNUNCIATION OF THE LORD
• Is 7:10-14; 8:10 • Ps 40:7-11 • Heb 10:4-10 • Lk 1:26-38

_____
_____
_____
_____
_____
_____
_____
_____
_____

26
Wednesday

• Dt 4:1, 5-9 • Ps 147:12-13, 15-16, 19-20 • Mt 5:17-19

_____
_____
_____
_____
_____
_____
_____
_____
_____

Lent reminds us, as St. Paul exhorts, "not to accept the grace of God in vain" (2 Corinthians 6:1), but to recognize that today the Lord calls us to penance and spiritual renewal.

—Pope Benedict XVI

• Jer 7:23-28 • Ps 95:1-2, 6-9 • Lk 11:14-23

27
Thursday

_____

_____

_____

_____

_____

_____

_____

_____

_____

_____

• Hos 14:2-10 • Ps 81:6c-11b, 14, 17 • Mk 12:28-34

28
Friday

_____

_____

_____

_____

_____

_____

_____

_____

_____

_____

MARCH

We must accept the cross with more gratitude than anything else. Our crosses detach us from earth and therefore draw us closer to God.

—**Blessed Charles de Foucauld**

29
Saturday

• Hos 6:1-6 • Ps 51:3-4, 18-21b • Lk 18:9-14

_____
_____
_____
_____
_____
_____
_____
_____
_____

30
Sunday

FOURTH SUNDAY OF LENT
• 1 Sm 16:1b, 6-7, 10-13a • Ps 23:1-6 • Eph 5:8-14 • Jn 9:1-41

_____
_____
_____
_____
_____
_____
_____
_____
_____

We Need Your Help!

Dear Friend in Christ,

Below is a survey form to help us know how to best meet your needs and interests in future editions of the *Prayer Journal*. Please take a moment and answer the following questions. In gratitude for your completed survey, we will take 10% off the price of your *Prayer Journal* for the next year!

1) In your use of the *Prayer Journal,* what features are essential to include? (Check as many responses as you find relevant and/or important to you personally.)

☐ The daily Mass readings citations

☐ Designation of special holy days and saints' feast days

☐ Referencing the day of the week and the date of the month

☐ Inspiring spiritual quotation on each page

☐ Spiral binding

2) The *Prayer Journal's* particular theme for the year (this year it is "Draw Near to God") is an important factor in my decision to purchase it.

☐ Agree. The year's theme is important in my purchasing decision.

☐ Disagree. The year's theme has little impact on my purchasing decision.

3) Which of the above features listed in question #1 would you miss if they were not included in the journal?

_____

_____

4) Do you have any suggestions for improving the *Prayer Journal*?

_____

_____

5) Do you use the *Prayer Journal's* companion book, called *Abide in My Word: Mass Readings at Your Fingertips?*

☐ Yes   ☐ No

Thank you for completing our survey. To reserve next year's *Prayer Journal* at the reduced price, complete the form below and return to:

Prayer Journal Survey
The Word Among Us
7115 Guilford Drive, Suite 100
Frederick, MD 21704

☐ **YES!** Reserve _____ copies of next year's *Prayer Journal*.
I understand that I will receive 10% off each copy and therefore pay only $12.56 each, plus shipping and handling. I will not be billed until I receive my *Prayer Journal* in fall 2014.

JP2015

☐ **YES!** In addition, reserve _____ copies of next year's *Abide in My Word: Mass Readings at Your Fingertips*. I will receive 10% off each copy, therefore paying only $14.85 each plus shipping and handling. I will not be billed until I receive my *Abide* in fall 2014.

AB2015

Name _____

Address _____

City _____

State _____ Zip _____

Country _____

Phone (_____) _____

E-mail _____

NOTE: Only surveys returned by <u>May 31, 2014</u>, will be eligible for this discount.

QUESTIONS?
Call *The Word Among Us* Customer Service at 1-800-775-WORD (9673) if you have any questions about this discount offer.

SHIPPING & HANDLING (Add to total product order):					
If your subtotal is:	$0-15	$16-$35	$36-50	$51-75	$76-100
Add shipping of:	$5	$7	$9	$11	$13

CPPJ14S

You can pray by putting yourself quite simply in touch with God. When one finds nothing more to say to him but just knows he is there—that in itself is the best of prayers.

—**St. John Vianney**

• Is 65:17-21 • Ps 30:2, 4-6, 11-13b • Jn 4:43-54

31
Monday

M ARCH

APRIL

O Lord, whose way is perfect, help us, we pray, always to trust in your goodness, that walking with you and following you in all simplicity, we may possess quiet and contented minds and may cast all our cares on you, who cares for us. Grant this, O Lord, for your dear Son's sake, Jesus Christ. Amen.

—*Christina Rossetti*

Love above all else our merciful Father in heaven, and serve him
with all your strength and purity of heart.

—St. Francis of Paola

1
Tuesday

• Ez 47:1-9, 12 • Ps 46:2-3, 5-6, 8-9 • Jn 5:1-16

_____

_____

_____

_____

_____

_____

_____

_____

_____

2
Wednesday

SAINT FRANCIS OF PAOLA
• Is 49:8-15 • Ps 145:8-9, 13c-14, 17-18 • Jn 5:17-30

_____

_____

_____

_____

_____

_____

_____

_____

_____

> Speak now, my heart, and say to God, "I seek your face;
> your face, Lord, I seek."
>
> —St. Anselm

• Ex 32:7-14 • Ps 106:19-23 • Jn 5:31-47

3
Thursday

_____
_____
_____
_____
_____
_____
_____
_____
_____

SAINT ISIDORE
• Wis 2:1a, 12-22 • Ps 34:17-21, 23 • Jn 7:1-2, 10, 25-30

4
Friday

_____
_____
_____
_____
_____
_____
_____
_____
_____

APRIL

When the soul has seen God, what more can it want?
If it possesses him, why and for whom can it ever be moved
to abandon him?

—St. Vincent Ferrer

5
Saturday

SAINT VINCENT FERRER
• Jer 11:18-20 • Ps 7:2-3, 9b-12 • Jn 7:40-53

_____

_____

_____

_____

_____

_____

_____

_____

_____

6
Sunday

FIFTH SUNDAY OF LENT
• Ez 37:12-14 • Ps 130:1-8 • Rom 8:8-11 • Jn 11:1-45

_____

_____

_____

_____

_____

_____

_____

_____

_____

> Be driven by the love of God then, because Jesus Christ died
> for all, that those who live may live not for themselves but for
> him who died and rose for them.
>
> —**St. John Baptist de la Salle**

SAINT JOHN BAPTIST DE LA SALLE
• Dn 13:1-9, 15-17, 19-30, 33-62 • Ps 23:1-6 • Jn 8:1-11

7
Monday

_____

_____

_____

_____

_____

_____

_____

_____

_____

• Nm 21:4-9 • Ps 102:2-3, 16-21 • Jn 8:21-30

8
Tuesday

_____

_____

_____

_____

_____

_____

_____

_____

_____

APRIL

All who worship the Lord, bless the God of gods,
sing praise to him and give thanks to him.

—Daniel 3:90

9
Wednesday

• Dn 3:14-20, 91-92, 95 • (Ps) Dn 3:52-56 • Jn 8:31-42

_____

_____

_____

_____

_____

_____

_____

_____

_____

10
Thursday

• Gn 17:3-9 • Ps 105:4-9 • Jn 8:51-59

_____

_____

_____

_____

_____

_____

_____

_____

_____

> Nowhere, perhaps, has our divine Savior more clearly
> and forcibly spoken of himself as both God and man as in
> the days of his passion.
>
> **—Blessed Columba Marmion**

SAINT STANISLAUS
• Jer 20:10-13 • Ps 18:2-7 • Jn 10:31-42

11
Friday

_____
_____
_____
_____
_____
_____
_____
_____
_____

• Ez 37:21-28 • (Ps) Jer 31:10-13 • Jn 11:45-56

12
Saturday

_____
_____
_____
_____
_____
_____
_____
_____
_____

APRIL

Jesus' entry into Jerusalem manifests the coming of the kingdom that the Messiah-King . . . is going to accomplish by the Passover of his death and resurrection.

—Catechism of the Catholic Church, **570**

13
Sunday

PALM SUNDAY OF THE PASSION OF THE LORD
• Mt 21:1-11 • Is 50:4-7 • Ps 22:8-9, 17-20, 23-24 • Phil 2:6-11
• Mt 26:14–27:66

_____

_____

_____

_____

_____

_____

_____

_____

14
Monday

MONDAY OF HOLY WEEK
• Is 42:1-7 • Ps 27:1-3, 13-14 • Jn 12:1-11

_____

_____

_____

_____

_____

_____

_____

_____

_____

We are going to commemorate the passion of our Savior;
let us strive to prepare ourselves for it by great purity of heart.
—St. Jane Frances de Chantal

TUESDAY OF HOLY WEEK
• Is 49:1-6 • Ps 71:1-6b, 15, 17 • Jn 13:21-33, 36-38

15
Tuesday

_____

_____

_____

_____

_____

_____

_____

_____

_____

WEDNESDAY OF HOLY WEEK
• Is 50:4-9a • Ps 69:8-10, 21-22, 31, 33-34 • Mt 26:14-25

16
Wednesday

_____

_____

_____

_____

_____

_____

_____

_____

_____

_____

APRIL

As an eagle, the Lord spreads his wings over us, his nestlings. . . .
He will be lifted up on the cross; he will stretch forth
his hands to shelter us.

—St. Jerome

17
Thursday

HOLY THURSDAY
• Ex 12:1-8, 11-14 • Ps 116:12-13, 15-18 • 1 Cor 11:23-26 • Jn 13:1-15

_____

_____

_____

_____

_____

_____

_____

_____

18
Friday

FRIDAY OF THE PASSION OF THE LORD (GOOD FRIDAY)
• Is 52:13–53:12 • Ps 31:2, 6, 12-13, 15-17, 25 • Heb 4:14-16; 5:7-9
• Jn 18:1–19:42

_____

_____

_____

_____

_____

_____

_____

_____

_____

Today is indeed the Lord's own Passover, for from death to life, from earth to heaven, Christ has led us as we shout the victory hymn! Christ has risen from the dead!

—**St. John of Damascus**

HOLY SATURDAY (EASTER VIGIL)

19
Saturday

- Gn 1:1–2:2 • Gn 22:1-18 • Ex 14:15–15:1 • Is 54:5-14 • Is 55:1-11
- Bar 3:9-15, 32–4:4 • Ez 36:16-17a, 18-28 • Rom 6:3-11
- Ps 118:1-2, 16-17, 22-23 • Mt 28:1-10

_____

_____

_____

_____

_____

_____

_____

_____

_____

_____

EASTER SUNDAY OF THE RESURRECTION OF THE LORD

20
Sunday

- Acts 10:34a, 37-43 • Ps 118:1-2, 16-17, 22-23 •
Col 3:1-4 or 1 Cor 5:6b-8 • Jn 20:1-9 or Mt 28:1-10

_____

_____

_____

_____

_____

_____

_____

_____

_____

APRIL

Easter is a feast of joy—the joy of the Lord. Let nothing so disturb us, so fill us with sorrow or discouragement, as to make us forfeit the joy of the resurrection.

—**Blessed Teresa of Calcutta**

21 Monday

MONDAY WITHIN THE OCTAVE OF EASTER
• Acts 2:14, 22-33 • Ps 16:1-2a, 5, 7-11 • Mt 28:8-15

_____

_____

_____

_____

_____

_____

_____

_____

_____

22 Tuesday

TUESDAY WITHIN THE OCTAVE OF EASTER
• Acts 2:36-41 • Ps 33:4-5, 18-20, 22 • Jn 20:11-18

_____

_____

_____

_____

_____

_____

_____

_____

_____

> The confidence of Christians is in the resurrection of the dead;
> believing this we live.
>
> **—Tertullian**

WEDNESDAY WITHIN THE OCTAVE OF EASTER
• Acts 3:1-10 • Ps 105:1-4, 6-9 • Lk 24:13-35

23
Wednesday

_____

_____

_____

_____

_____

_____

_____

_____

_____

_____

THURSDAY WITHIN THE OCTAVE OF EASTER
• Acts 3:11-26 • Ps 8:2, 5-9 • Lk 24:35-48

24
Thursday

_____

_____

_____

_____

_____

_____

_____

_____

_____

_____

APRIL

I thank you that you have answered me
and have become my salvation.

—**Psalm 118:21**

25
Friday

FRIDAY WITHIN THE OCTAVE OF EASTER
• Acts 4:1-12 • Ps 118:1-2, 4, 22-27a • Jn 21:1-14

_____

_____

_____

_____

_____

_____

_____

_____

_____

26
Saturday

SATURDAY WITHIN THE OCTAVE OF EASTER
• Acts 4:13-21 • Ps 118:1, 14-21 • Mk 16:9-15

_____

_____

_____

_____

_____

_____

_____

_____

_____

Rich is the mercy of our God, and abundantly does he bestow
grace upon grace on those who love him.

—St. Elizabeth of Schönau

SECOND SUNDAY OF EASTER OR SUNDAY OF DIVINE MERCY

27
Sunday

• Acts 2:42-47 • Ps 118:2-4, 13-15, 22-24 • 1 Pt 1:3-9 • Jn 20:19-31

_____
_____
_____
_____
_____
_____
_____
_____
_____
_____

SAINT PETER CHANEL; SAINT LOUIS DE MONTFORT

28
Monday

• Acts 4:23-31 • Ps 2:1-9 • Jn 3:1-8

_____
_____
_____
_____
_____
_____
_____
_____
_____
_____

APRIL

Build yourself a cell in your heart and retire there to pray.
—St. Catherine of Siena

29
Tuesday

SAINT CATHERINE OF SIENA
• Acts 4:32-37 • Ps 93:1-2, 5 • Jn 3:7b-15

_____

_____

_____

_____

_____

_____

_____

_____

_____

30
Wednesday

SAINT PIUS V
• Acts 5:17-26 • Ps 34:2-9 • Jn 3:16-21

_____

_____

_____

_____

_____

_____

_____

_____

_____

O my Lord Jesus Christ crucified, Son of the most blessed Virgin Mary, open your arms and embrace me as you opened them upon the cross to embrace the whole human race.

—St. Pius V

_____

_____

_____

_____

_____

_____

_____

_____

_____

_____

_____

_____

_____

_____

_____

_____

_____

_____

_____

_____

_____

_____

_____

_____

_____

APRIL

MAY

Virgin Mother of God,
we, the peoples of all nations,
proclaim you blessed;
he, who surpasses all things,
Christ, our God, in you has deigned to dwell.
Blessed are we,
who have you as our defense,
for you intercede night and day for us. . . .
And so we hymn our praise to you, proclaiming:
Hail, full of grace, the Lord is with you.

—Sixth-Century Hymn

All for Jesus, all for Mary, all after your example, O patriarch Joseph. Such shall be my watchword in life and death. Amen.

—St. Pius X

1
Thursday

SAINT JOSEPH THE WORKER
• Acts 5:27-33 • Ps 34:2, 9, 17-20 • Jn 3:31-36 (or for the memorial of St. Joseph the Worker: • Gn 1:26–2:3 or Col 3:14-15, 17, 23-24
• Ps 98:1-4 or Ps 90:2-4, 12-14, 16 • Mt 13:54-58)

2
Friday

SAINT ATHANASIUS
• Acts 5:34-42 • Ps 27:1, 4, 13-14 • Jn 6:1-15

> Like every good evangelist, Philip not only spoke to others about Christ but invited them to meet him personally.
>
> **—Pope Benedict XVI**

SAINTS PHILIP AND JAMES, APOSTLES
• 1 Cor 15:1-8 • Ps 19:2-5 • Jn 14:6-14

3
Saturday

_____
_____
_____
_____
_____
_____
_____
_____
_____

THIRD SUNDAY OF EASTER
• Acts 2:14, 22-33 • Ps 16:1-2, 5, 7-11 • 1 Pt 1:17-21 • Lk 24:13-35

4
Sunday

_____
_____
_____
_____
_____
_____
_____
_____
_____

M A Y

Pray with great confidence, . . . based upon the goodness and infinite generosity of God and upon the promises of Jesus Christ. God is a spring of living water which flows unceasingly into the hearts of those who pray. —**St. Louis de Montfort**

5
Monday

• Acts 6:8-15 • Ps 119:23-24, 26-27, 29-30 • Jn 6:22-29

_____

_____

_____

_____

_____

_____

_____

_____

_____

6
Tuesday

• Acts 7:51–8:1a • Ps 31:3c-4, 6-8a, 17, 21ab • Jn 6:30-35

_____

_____

_____

_____

_____

_____

_____

_____

_____

My Jesus, how good it is to love you! Let us be as two friends, neither of whom can ever bear to offend the other.

—St. John Vianney

• Acts 8:1b-8 • Ps 66:1-7a • Jn 6:35-40

_____

_____

_____

_____

_____

_____

_____

_____

_____

• Acts 8:26-40 • Ps 66:8-9, 16-17, 20 • Jn 6:44-51

_____

_____

_____

_____

_____

_____

_____

_____

_____

M A Y

Holy Communion keeps me full of joy. . . . I find my
consolation in my only Companion, who never leaves me.

—St. Damien de Veuster

9 Friday
• Acts 9:1-20 • Ps 117:1b-2 • Jn 6:52-59

_____

_____

_____

_____

_____

_____

_____

_____

_____

10 Saturday
SAINT DAMIEN DE VEUSTER
• Acts 9:31-42 • Ps 116:12-17 • Jn 6:60-69

_____

_____

_____

_____

_____

_____

_____

_____

_____

Both humility and prayer grow from an ear, mind, and tongue that have lived in silence with God, for in the silence of the heart God speaks.

—Blessed Teresa of Calcutta

FOURTH SUNDAY OF EASTER
• Acts 2:14a, 36-41 • Ps 23:1-6 • 1 Pt 2:20b-25 • Jn 10:1-10

11
Sunday

_____
_____
_____
_____
_____
_____
_____
_____
_____
_____

SAINTS NEREUS AND ACHILLEUS; SAINT PANCRAS
• Acts 11:1-18 • Ps 42:2-3; 43:3-4 • Jn 10:11-18

12
Monday

_____
_____
_____
_____
_____
_____
_____
_____
_____
_____

M A Y

To recite the Rosary is nothing other than to contemplate
with Mary the face of Christ.

—Blessed John Paul II

13
Tuesday

OUR LADY OF FATIMA
• Acts 11:19-26 • Ps 87:1b-7 • Jn 10:22-30

_____

_____

_____

_____

_____

_____

_____

_____

14
Wednesday

SAINT MATTHIAS, APOSTLE
• Acts 1:15-17, 20-26 • Ps 113:1-8 • Jn 15:9-17

_____

_____

_____

_____

_____

_____

_____

_____

_____

I am the way, and the truth, and the life. No one comes
to the Father except through me.

—**Jesus in John 14:6**

SAINT ISIDORE
• Acts 13:13-25 • Ps 89:2-3, 21-22, 25, 27 • Jn 13:16-20

15
Thursday

_____

_____

_____

_____

_____

_____

_____

_____

_____

• Acts 13:26-33 • Ps 2:6-11b • Jn 14:1-6

16
Friday

_____

_____

_____

_____

_____

_____

_____

_____

MAY

What an extraordinary thing it is, the efficiency of prayer!
Like a queen, it has access at all times to the royal Presence,
and can get whatever it asks for.

—St. Thérèse of Lisieux

17
Saturday
• Acts 13:44-52 • Ps 98:1-4 • Jn 14:7-14

_____

_____

_____

_____

_____

_____

_____

_____

_____

18
Sunday
FIFTH SUNDAY OF EASTER
• Acts 6:1-7 • Ps 33:1-2, 4-5, 18-19 • 1 Pt 2:4-9 • Jn 14:1-12

_____

_____

_____

_____

_____

_____

_____

_____

_____

_____

The Name of Jesus is the most sweet-tasting nourishment
of contemplation, for it feeds and revives those souls that are
famished and spiritually hungry.

—**St. Bernardine of Siena**

• Acts 14:5-18 • Ps 115:1-4, 15-16 • Jn 14:21-26

19
Monday

_____

_____

_____

_____

_____

_____

_____

_____

_____

_____

SAINT BERNARDINE OF SIENA
• Acts 14:19-28 • Ps 145:10-13b, 21 • Jn 14:27-31a

20
Tuesday

_____

_____

_____

_____

_____

_____

_____

_____

_____

M A Y

> O loving Jesus, increase my patience according
> as my sufferings increase.
>
> —**St. Rita of Cascia**

21
Wednesday

SAINT CHRISTOPHER MAGALLANES AND COMPANIONS
• Acts 15:1-6 • Ps 122:1-5 • Jn 15:1-8

_____

_____

_____

_____

_____

_____

_____

_____

22
Thursday

SAINT RITA OF CASCIA
• Acts 15:7-21 • Ps 96:1-3, 10 • Jn 15:9-11

_____

_____

_____

_____

_____

_____

_____

_____

Make a joyful noise to the LORD, all the earth.
Worship the LORD with gladness;
come into his presence with singing.

—Psalm 100:1-2

• Acts 15:22-31 • Ps 57:8-10, 12 • Jn 15:12-17

23
Friday

_____
_____
_____
_____
_____
_____
_____
_____
_____

• Acts 16:1-10 • Ps 100:1b-3, 5 • Jn 15:18-21

24
Saturday

_____
_____
_____
_____
_____
_____
_____
_____
_____

MAY

My Jesus, if you do not uphold me, I shall fall.
My Jesus, if you do not help me, I am ruined.

—**St. Philip Neri**

25 Sunday

SIXTH SUNDAY OF EASTER
• Acts 8:5-8, 14-17 • Ps 66:1-7, 16, 20 • 1 Pt 3:15-18 • Jn 14:15-21

_____

_____

_____

_____

_____

_____

_____

_____

_____

26 Monday

SAINT PHILIP NERI
• Acts 16:11-15 • Ps 149:1b-6a, 9b • Jn 15:26–16:4a

_____

_____

_____

_____

_____

_____

_____

_____

_____

Praise the Lord!
Praise the Lord from the heavens;
praise him in the heights!

—Psalm 148:1

Saint Augustine of Canterbury
• Acts 16:22-34 • Ps 138:1-3, 7c-8 • Jn 16:5-11

27
Tuesday

_____
_____
_____
_____
_____
_____
_____
_____
_____

• Acts 17:15, 22–18:1 • Ps 148:1-2, 11-14 • Jn 16:12-15

28
Wednesday

_____
_____
_____
_____
_____
_____
_____
_____
_____

M A Y

Christ has gone to heaven, and at the same time he gives himself
to us as our nourishment in the sacred host.
—**St. Josemaría Escrivá**

29
Thursday

• Acts 18:1-8 • Ps 98:1, 4 • Jn 16:16-20
OR THE ASCENSION OF THE LORD
• Acts 1:1-11 • Ps 47:2-3, 6-9 • Eph 1:17-23 • Mt 28:16-20

_____

_____

_____

_____

_____

_____

_____

_____

30
Friday

• Acts 18:9-18 • Ps 47:2-7 • Jn 16:20-23

_____

_____

_____

_____

_____

_____

_____

_____

_____

Let the soul of Mary be in each of us to magnify the Lord, and the spirit of Mary be in each of us to rejoice in God.

—St. Anselm

THE VISITATION OF THE BLESSED VIRGIN MARY
• Zep 3:14-18a or Rom 12:9-16 • (Ps) Is 12:2-6 • Lk 1:39-56

31
Saturday

M A Y

JUNE

O Sacred Heart of Jesus, living and quicken-
ing source of eternal life, infinite treasury of the
divinity, burning furnace of divine love—you are
my refuge and my sanctuary. . . . Let my heart be
so united with yours that our wills may be one—
that in all things my will may be conformed to
yours, that your will may be the standard and rule
of my desires and my actions. Amen.

—*St. Gertrude*

God our Father, make us joyful in the ascension of your Son Jesus Christ. May we follow him into the new creation, for his ascension is our glory and our hope.

—**Ascension Evening Prayer,** *Liturgy of the Hours*

1
Sunday

THE ASCENSION OF THE LORD
• Acts 1:1-11 • Ps 47:2-3, 6-9 • Eph 1:17-23 • Mt 28:16-20

OR SEVENTH SUNDAY OF EASTER
• Acts 1:12-14 • Ps 27:1, 4, 7-8 • 1 Pt 4:13-16 • Jn 17:1-11a

_____

_____

_____

_____

_____

_____

_____

_____

2
Monday

SAINTS MARCELLINUS AND PETER
• Acts 19:1-8 • Ps 68:2-7b • Jn 16:29-33

_____

_____

_____

_____

_____

_____

_____

_____

_____

The death of the martyrs blossoms in the faith of the living.
—**Pope St. Gregory the Great**

SAINT CHARLES LWANGA AND COMPANIONS
• Acts 20:17-27 • Ps 68:10-11, 20-21 • Jn 17:1-11a

3
Tuesday

• Acts 20:28-38 • Ps 68:29-30, 33-36b • Jn 17:11b-19

4
Wednesday

JUNE

Listen cheerfully to the word of God, keep it
judiciously and observe it faithfully.

—**St. Norbert**

5
Thursday

SAINT BONIFACE
• Acts 22:30; 23:6-11 • Ps 16:1-2a, 5, 7-11 • Jn 17:20-26

_____

_____

_____

_____

_____

_____

_____

_____

_____

6
Friday

SAINT NORBERT
• Acts 25:13b-21 • Ps 103:1-2, 11-12, 19-20b • Jn 21:15-19

_____

_____

_____

_____

_____

_____

_____

_____

_____

Rejoicing and eternal praise be to you, my Lord Jesus Christ,
who sent the Holy Spirit into the hearts of your disciples.

—St. Bridget of Sweden

• Acts 28:16-20, 30-31 • Ps 11:4-5, 7 • Jn 21:20-25

7
Saturday

_____

_____

_____

_____

_____

_____

_____

_____

_____

PENTECOST SUNDAY
• Acts 2:1-11 • Ps 104:1, 24, 29-31, 34 • 1 Cor 12:3b-7, 12-13
• Jn 20:19-23

8
Sunday

_____

_____

_____

_____

_____

_____

_____

_____

_____

JUNE

> Let us offer the Lord the great and all-encompassing
> sacrifice of our love, pouring out the treasury
> of hymns and prayers before him.
>
> —St. Ephrem

9
Monday

SAINT EPHREM
• 1 Kgs 17:1-6 • Ps 121:1b-8 • Mt 5:1-12

_____

_____

_____

_____

_____

_____

_____

_____

10
Tuesday

• 1 Kgs 17:7-16 • Ps 4:2-5, 7b-8 • Mt 5:13-16

_____

_____

_____

_____

_____

_____

_____

_____

_____

While they were worshipping the Lord and fasting,
the Holy Spirit said, "Set apart for me Barnabas and Saul for
the work to which I have called them."

—Acts 13:2

SAINT BARNABAS, APOSTLE
• Acts 11:21b-26; 13:1-3 • Ps 98:1-6 • Mt 5:17-19

11
Wednesday

_____

_____

_____

_____

_____

_____

_____

_____

_____

• 1 Kgs 18:41-46 • Ps 65:10-13 • Mt 5:20-26

12
Thursday

_____

_____

_____

_____

_____

_____

_____

_____

_____

JUNE

> O the mercy of God! Never does he refuse to be merciful, but is ever present to those who turn to him.

—St. Anthony of Padua

13
Friday

SAINT ANTHONY OF PADUA
• 1 Kgs 19:9a, 11-16 • Ps 27:7-9, 13-14 • Mt 5:27-32

_____

_____

_____

_____

_____

_____

_____

_____

14
Saturday

• 1 Kgs 19:19-21 • Ps 16:1b-2a, 5, 7-10 • Mt 5:33-37

_____

_____

_____

_____

_____

_____

_____

_____

_____

My God, Blessed Trinity! Draw from my poor being
what most contributes to your glory, and do with me what
you wish, both now and in eternity.

—Blessed Elizabeth of the Trinity

THE MOST HOLY TRINITY

• Ex 34:4b-6, 8-9 • (Ps) Dn 3:52-56 • 2 Cor 13:11-13 • Jn 3:16-18

15
Sunday

_____

_____

_____

_____

_____

_____

_____

_____

• 1 Kgs 21:1-16 • Ps 5:2-7 • Mt 5:38-42

16
Monday

_____

_____

_____

_____

_____

_____

_____

_____

JUNE

Blessed be the LORD,
for he has wondrously shown his steadfast love to me.

—**Psalm 31:21**

17
Tuesday

• 1 Kgs 21:17-29 • Ps 51:3-6b, 11, 16 • Mt 5:43-48

_____

_____

_____

_____

_____

_____

_____

_____

18
Wednesday

• 2 Kgs 2:1, 6-14 • Ps 31:20-21, 24 • Mt 6:1-6, 16-18

_____

_____

_____

_____

_____

_____

_____

_____

> Beloved Jesus, beloved, sweet honey, indescribable longing,
> delight of the saints, sweetness of the angels!
>
> —**St. Romuald**

SAINT ROMUALD
• Sir 48:1-14 • Ps 97:1-7 • Mt 6:7-15

19
Thursday

_____
_____
_____
_____
_____
_____
_____
_____
_____

• 2 Kgs 11:1-4, 9-18, 20 • Ps 132:11-14, 17-18 • Mt 6:19-23

20
Friday

_____
_____
_____
_____
_____
_____
_____
_____

JUNE

If you wish to adore the real face of Jesus, we can find it in the divine Eucharist, where with the body and blood of Jesus Christ, the face of our Lord is hidden under the white veil of the host.

—St. Gaetano Catanoso

21
Saturday

SAINT ALOYSIUS GONZAGA
• 2 Chr 24:17-25 • Ps 89:4-5, 29-34 • Mt 6:24-34

_____

_____

_____

_____

_____

_____

_____

_____

_____

22
Sunday

THE MOST HOLY BODY AND BLOOD OF CHRIST
(CORPUS CHRISTI)
• Dt 8:2-3, 14b-16a • Ps 147:12-15, 19-20 • 1 Cor 10:16-17 • Jn 6:51-58

_____

_____

_____

_____

_____

_____

_____

_____

Look today to John the Baptist, an enduring model
of fidelity to God and his law. . . . Imitate him with docile
and trusting generosity.

—**Blessed John Paul II**

• 2 Kgs 17:5-8, 13-15a, 18 • Ps 60:3-5, 12-13 • Mt 7:1-5

23
Monday

_____

_____

_____

_____

_____

_____

_____

_____

_____

THE NATIVITY OF SAINT JOHN THE BAPTIST
• Is 49:1-6 • Ps 139:1b-3, 13-15 • Acts 13:22-26 • Lk 1:57-66, 80

24
Tuesday

_____

_____

_____

_____

_____

_____

_____

_____

J UNE

We follow him and he draws us to himself by love. . . .
Prayer makes the soul one with God.

—Julian of Norwich

25
Wednesday

• 2 Kgs 22:8-13; 23:1-3 • Ps 119:33-37, 40 • Mt 7:15-20

_____
_____
_____
_____
_____
_____
_____
_____
_____

26
Thursday

• 2 Kgs 24:8-17 • Ps 79:1b-5, 8-9 • Mt 7:21-29

_____
_____
_____
_____
_____
_____
_____
_____
_____

The adorable Heart of Jesus Christ began to beat
with a love at once human and divine after the Virgin Mary
generously pronounced her *fiat*.

—**Pope Pius XII**

THE MOST SACRED HEART OF JESUS
• Dt 7:6-11 • Ps 103:1-4, 6-8, 10 • 1 Jn 4:7-16 • Mt 11:25-30

27
Friday

_____
_____
_____
_____
_____
_____
_____
_____
_____
_____

THE IMMACULATE HEART OF THE BLESSED VIRGIN MARY
• Lam 2:2, 10-14, 18-19 • Ps 74:1b-7, 20-21 • Lk 2:41-51

28
Saturday

_____
_____
_____
_____
_____
_____
_____
_____
_____
_____

JUNE

May the example of the apostles Peter and Paul illumine minds and kindle in the hearts of believers the holy desire to do God's will, so that the pilgrim Church on this earth may always be faithful to her Lord. —**Pope Benedict XVI**

29
Sunday

SAINTS PETER AND PAUL, APOSTLES
• Acts 12:1-11 • Ps 34:2-9 • 2 Tm 4:6-8, 17-18 • Mt 16:13-19

_____
_____
_____
_____
_____
_____
_____
_____
_____

30
Monday

THE FIRST MARTYRS OF THE HOLY ROMAN CHURCH
• Am 2:6-10, 13-16 • Ps 50:16b-23 • Mt 8:18-22

_____
_____
_____
_____
_____
_____
_____
_____
_____

May your faith be increased so as to realize the fact
that you are never alone, wheresoever you may be, that the
great God is with you, in you.

—St. Katharine Drexel

_____

_____

_____

_____

_____

_____

_____

_____

_____

_____

_____

_____

_____

_____

_____

_____

_____

_____

_____

_____

_____

_____

_____

_____

_____

JUNE

JULY

Take, O Lord, and receive all my liberty, my memory, my understanding, and my whole will. You have given me all that I am and all that I possess; I surrender it all to you that you may dispose of it according to your will. Give me only your love and your grace; with these I will be rich enough, and will have no more to desire. Amen.

—St. Ignatius of Loyola

All my life, I have . . . wanted to carry the gospel message
to those who have never heard of God.
—**Blessed Junípero Serra**

1
Tuesday

BLESSED JUNÍPERO SERRA
• Am 3:1-8; 4:11-12 • Ps 5:4b-8 • Mt 8:23-27

_____

_____

_____

_____

_____

_____

_____

_____

_____

2
Wednesday

• Am 5:14-15, 21-24 • Ps 50:7-13, 16b-17 • Mt 8:28-34

_____

_____

_____

_____

_____

_____

_____

_____

_____

There is something of the apostle Thomas in every human being. Each one is tempted by unbelief. . . . We have to open our eyes and our heart to the light of the Holy Spirit.

—Blessed John Paul II

SAINT THOMAS, APOSTLE
• Eph 2:19-22 • Ps 117:1b-2 • Jn 20:24-29

3
Thursday

_____
_____
_____
_____
_____
_____
_____
_____
_____
_____

INDEPENDENCE DAY (USA)
• Am 8:4-6, 9-12 • Ps 119:2, 10, 20, 30, 40, 131 • Mt 9:9-13

4
Friday

_____
_____
_____
_____
_____
_____
_____
_____
_____
_____

JULY

Let us not lose sight of Jesus, who endured the cross, . . .
and we shall prove that we are servants of God by great
fortitude in times of suffering.

—St. Anthony Zaccaria

5
Saturday

SAINT ANTHONY ZACCARIA;
SAINT ELIZABETH OF PORTUGAL
• Am 9:11-15 • Ps 85:9ab, 10-14 • Mt 9:14-17

_____

_____

_____

_____

_____

_____

_____

_____

6
Sunday

FOURTEENTH SUNDAY IN ORDINARY TIME
• Zec 9:9-10 • Ps 145:1-2, 8-11, 13-14 • Rom 8:9, 11-13 • Mt 11:25-30

_____

_____

_____

_____

_____

_____

_____

_____

Prayer coming forth from a clean conscience is like
the incense of sweetness in heaven.

—St. Elizabeth of Schönau

• Hos 2:16, 17c-18, 21-22 • Ps 145:2-9 • Mt 9:18-26

7
Monday

_____
_____
_____
_____
_____
_____
_____
_____
_____

• Hos 8:4-7, 11-13 • Ps 115:3-10 • Mt 9:32-38

8
Tuesday

_____
_____
_____
_____
_____
_____
_____
_____
_____

JULY

Martyrdom is the supreme witness given to the truth of the faith:
it means bearing witness even unto death.

—*Catechism of the Catholic Church,* **2473**

9
Wednesday

SAINT AUGUSTINE ZHAO RONG AND COMPANIONS
• Hos 10:1-3, 7-8, 12 • Ps 105:2-7 • Mt 10:1-7

10
Thursday

• Hos 11:1-4, 8e-9 • Ps 80:2-3b, 15-16 • Mt 10:7-15

> What is more delightful than this voice of the Lord calling to us?
> See how the Lord in his love shows us the way of life.
>
> **—St. Benedict**

SAINT BENEDICT
• Hos 14:2-10 • Ps 51:3-4, 8-9, 12-14, 17 • Mt 10:16-23

11
Friday

_____
_____
_____
_____
_____
_____
_____
_____
_____

• Is 6:1-8 • Ps 93:1-2, 5 • Mt 10:24-33

12
Saturday

_____
_____
_____
_____
_____
_____
_____
_____
_____

JULY

> Who can tell me what is most pleasing to God, that I may do it?
> —**St. Kateri Tekakwitha's motto**

13 Sunday
FIFTEENTH SUNDAY IN ORDINARY TIME
• Is 55:10-11 • Ps 65:10-14 • Rom 8:18-23 • Mt 13:1-23

_____

_____

_____

_____

_____

_____

_____

_____

_____

14 Monday
SAINT KATERI TEKAKWITHA
• Is 1:10-17 • Ps 50:8-9, 16b-17, 21, 23 • Mt 10:34–11:1

_____

_____

_____

_____

_____

_____

_____

_____

_____

_____

When we pray, the voice of the heart must be heard more
than the proceedings from the mouth.

—**St. Bonaventure**

SAINT BONAVENTURE
• Is 7:1-9 • Ps 48:2-8 • Mt 11:20-24

15
Tuesday

_____

_____

_____

_____

_____

_____

_____

_____

_____

OUR LADY OF MOUNT CARMEL
• Is 10:5-7, 13b-16 • Ps 94:5-10, 14-15 • Mt 11:25-27

16
Wednesday

_____

_____

_____

_____

_____

_____

_____

_____

_____

_____

JULY

My soul yearns for you in the night,
my spirit within me earnestly seeks you.

—**Isaiah 26:9**

17
Thursday

• Is 26:7-9, 12, 16-19 • Ps 102:13-21 • Mt 11:28-30

_____

_____

_____

_____

_____

_____

_____

_____

_____

18
Friday

SAINT CAMILLUS DE LELLIS
• Is 38:1-6, 21-22, 7-8 • (Ps) Is 38:10-12, 16 • Mt 12:1-8

_____

_____

_____

_____

_____

_____

_____

_____

_____

> Prayer is the raising of the mind to God. We must always remember this. The actual words matter less.
>
> —**Blessed John XXIII**

• Mi 2:1-5 • Ps 10:1-4, 7-8, 14 • Mt 12:14-21

19
Saturday

_____
_____
_____
_____
_____
_____
_____
_____
_____

SIXTEENTH SUNDAY IN ORDINARY TIME
• Wis 12:13, 16-19 • Ps 86:5-6, 9-10, 15-16 • Rom 8:26-27
• Mt 13:24-43

20
Sunday

_____
_____
_____
_____
_____
_____
_____
_____
_____

J ULY

When you feel invited to remain in silence at our Lord's feet like Magdalene, just looking at him with your heart, without saying anything . . . but just remain in loving adoration.

—Blessed Columba Marmion

21
Monday

SAINT LAWRENCE OF BRINDISI
• Mi 6:1-4, 6-8 • Ps 50:5-6, 8-9, 16b-17, 21, 23 • Mt 12:38-42

_____

_____

_____

_____

_____

_____

_____

_____

_____

22
Tuesday

SAINT MARY MAGDALENE
• Mi 7:14-15, 18-20 • Ps 85:2-8 • Jn 20:1-2, 11-18

_____

_____

_____

_____

_____

_____

_____

_____

_____

> May Saint Sharbel draw us after him along the path
> of sanctity, where silent prayer in the presence of God has
> its own particular place.
>
> **—Pope Paul VI**

SAINT BRIDGET
• Jer 1:1, 4-10 • Ps 71:1-6b, 15, 17 • Mt 13:1-9

23
Wednesday

_____
_____
_____
_____
_____
_____
_____
_____
_____
_____

SAINT SHARBEL MAKHLUF
• Jer 2:1-3, 7-8, 12-13 • Ps 36:6-11 • Mt 13:10-17

24
Thursday

_____
_____
_____
_____
_____
_____
_____
_____
_____
_____

JULY

Joachim and Anne, how blessed a couple! . . . At your hands
the Creator was offered a gift excelling all other gifts: a chaste
mother, who alone was worthy of him.

—St. John Damascene

25 Friday
SAINT JAMES, APOSTLE
• 2 Cor 4:7-15 • Ps 126:1b-6 • Mt 20:20-28

_____

_____

_____

_____

_____

_____

_____

_____

_____

26 Saturday
SAINTS JOACHIM AND ANNE, PARENTS OF THE
BLESSED VIRGIN MARY
• Jer 7:1-11 • Ps 84:3-6a, 8a, 11 • Mt 13:24-30

_____

_____

_____

_____

_____

_____

_____

_____

_____

> We know that all things work together for good for those who love God, who are called according to his purpose.
>
> —**Romans 8:28**

Seventeenth Sunday in Ordinary Time

• 1 Kgs 3:5, 7-12 • Ps 119:57, 72, 76-77, 127-130 • Rom 8:28-30
• Mt 13:44-52

27
Sunday

_____

_____

_____

_____

_____

_____

_____

_____

_____

_____

• Jer 13:1-11 • (Ps) Dt 32:18-21 • Mt 13:31-35

28
Monday

_____

_____

_____

_____

_____

_____

_____

_____

_____

_____

JULY

Teach us, Jesus, to treat you with the loving friendliness
of Martha, Mary, and Lazarus.

—**St. Josemaría Escrivá**

29
Tuesday

SAINT MARTHA
• Jer 14:17-22 • Ps 79:8, 9, 11, 13 • Jn 11:19-27 or Lk 10:38-42

_____
_____
_____
_____
_____
_____
_____
_____

30
Wednesday

SAINT PETER CHRYSOLOGUS
• Jer 15:10, 16-21 • Ps 59:2-4, 10-11, 17-18 • Mt 13:44-46

_____
_____
_____
_____
_____
_____
_____
_____

> Every fresh Communion is a new gift that Jesus Christ
> makes of himself.
>
> —St. Ignatius of Loyola

SAINT IGNATIUS OF LOYOLA
• Jer 18:1-6 • Ps 146:1b-6b • Mt 13:47-53

31
Thursday

_____

_____

_____

_____

_____

_____

_____

_____

_____

_____

_____

_____

_____

_____

_____

_____

_____

_____

_____

JULY

AUGUST

Breathe in me, O Holy Spirit,
that my thoughts may all be holy.
Act in me, O Holy Spirit,
that my work, too, may be holy.
Draw my heart, O Holy Spirit,
that I may love only what is holy.
Strengthen me, O Holy Spirit,
that I may defend all that is holy.
Guard me, then, O Holy Spirit,
that I always may be holy. Amen.

—St. Augustine

> Abide in the home . . . of God like his child, who knows
> nothing, does nothing, makes a mess of everything, but
> nevertheless lives in his goodness.
>
> —St. Peter Julian Eymard

1 Friday

SAINT ALPHONSUS LIGUORI
• Jer 26:1-9 • Ps 69:5, 8-10, 14 • Mt 13:54-58

_____

_____

_____

_____

_____

_____

_____

_____

2 Saturday

SAINT EUSEBIUS OF VERCELLI;
SAINT PETER JULIAN EYMARD
• Jer 26:11-16, 24 • Ps 69:15-16, 30-31, 33-34 • Mt 14:1-12

_____

_____

_____

_____

_____

_____

_____

_____

> The good God is everywhere, ready to hear your prayer.
> —St. John Vianney

EIGHTEENTH SUNDAY IN ORDINARY TIME
• Is 55:1-3 • Ps 145:8-9, 15-18 • Rom 8:35, 37-39 • Mt 14:13-21

3
Sunday

_____

_____

_____

_____

_____

_____

_____

_____

_____

_____

SAINT JOHN VIANNEY
• Jer 28:1-17 • Ps 119:29, 43, 79-80, 95, 102 • Mt 14:22-36

4
Monday

_____

_____

_____

_____

_____

_____

_____

_____

_____

_____

AUGUST

The glory that shone around the disciples on the mount of the Transfiguration prefigures the contemplation of God in eternity.

—Dionysius

5
Tuesday

THE DEDICATION OF THE BASILICA OF SAINT MARY MAJOR
• Jer 30:1-2, 12-15, 18-22 • Ps 102:16-23, 29 • Mt 14:22-36 or Mt 15:1-2, 10-14

_____

_____

_____

_____

_____

_____

_____

_____

6
Wednesday

THE TRANSFIGURATION OF THE LORD
• Dn 7:9-10, 13-14 • Ps 97:1-2, 5-6, 9 • 2 Pt 1:16-19 • Mt 17:1-9

_____

_____

_____

_____

_____

_____

_____

_____

One who governs his passions is master of the world.
We must either command them or be commanded by them.
—**St. Dominic**

SAINT SIXTUS II AND COMPANIONS; SAINT CAJETAN
• Jer 31:31-34 • Ps 51:12-15, 18-19 • Mt 16:13-23

7
Thursday

_____

_____

_____

_____

_____

_____

_____

_____

SAINT DOMINIC
• Na 2:1, 3; 3:1-3, 6-7 • (Ps) Dt 32:35c-36b, 39, 41 • Mt 16:24-28

8
Friday

_____

_____

_____

_____

_____

_____

_____

_____

_____

AUGUST

Just take everything exactly as it is, put it in God's hands,
and leave it with him. Then you will be able to
rest in him—really rest.
—St. Teresa Benedicta of the Cross (Edith Stein)

9
Saturday

SAINT TERESA BENEDICTA OF THE CROSS
(EDITH STEIN)
• Hb 1:12–2:4 • Ps 9:8-13 • Mt 17:14-20

_____

_____

_____

_____

_____

_____

_____

_____

_____

10
Sunday

NINETEENTH SUNDAY IN ORDINARY TIME
• 1 Kgs 19:9a, 11-13a • Ps 85:9-14 • Rom 9:1-5 • Mt 14:22-33

_____

_____

_____

_____

_____

_____

_____

_____

Look, look on Jesus, poor and crucified, look on this Holy One,
who for your love has died, and remember [that] . . . this Jesus,
whom you gaze upon, loves you most tenderly.

—St. Clare

SAINT CLARE
• Ez 1:2-5, 24-28c • Ps 148:1-2, 11-14 • Mt 17:22-27

11
Monday

_____

_____

_____

_____

_____

_____

_____

_____

_____

_____

SAINT JANE FRANCES DE CHANTAL
• Ez 2:8–3:4 • Ps 119:14, 24, 72, 103, 111, 131 • Mt 18:1-5, 10, 12-14

12
Tuesday

_____

_____

_____

_____

_____

_____

_____

_____

_____

_____

AUGUST

We praise and thank you, O God, through your Son Jesus Christ our Lord, through whom you have enlightened us by revealing the light that never fades.

—**St. Hippolytus**

13
Wednesday

SAINTS PONTIAN AND HIPPOLYTUS
• Ez 9:1-7; 10:18-22 • Ps 113:1-6 • Mt 18:15-20

_____

_____

_____

_____

_____

_____

_____

_____

14
Thursday

SAINT MAXIMILIAN KOLBE
• Ez 12:1-12 • Ps 78:56-59, 61-62 • Mt 18:21–19:1

_____

_____

_____

_____

_____

_____

_____

_____

The Solemnity of the Assumption . . . serves as a useful occasion for all believers to meditate on the true sense and value of human existence in view of eternity.

—Pope Benedict XVI

THE ASSUMPTION OF THE BLESSED VIRGIN MARY
• Rv 11:19a; 12:1-6a, 10ab • Ps 45:10-12, 16 • 1 Cor 15:20-27
• Lk 1:39-56 *Holy Day of Obligation*

15
Friday

_____
_____
_____
_____
_____
_____
_____
_____
_____

SAINT STEPHEN OF HUNGARY
• Ez 18:1-10, 13b, 30-32 • Ps 51:12-15, 18-19 • Mt 19:13-15

16
Saturday

_____
_____
_____
_____
_____
_____
_____
_____
_____
_____

AUGUST

The thirst of Christ is a gate of access to the mystery of God,
who is in fact made thirsty to satisfy our thirst, as one made
poor so that we might become rich. Yes, God is thirsty for our
faith and our love. —**Pope Benedict XVI**

17
Sunday

TWENTIETH SUNDAY IN ORDINARY TIME
• Is 56:1, 6-7 • Ps 67:2-3, 5-6, 8 • Rom 11:13-15, 29-32 • Mt 15:21-28

_____

_____

_____

_____

_____

_____

_____

_____

_____

18
Monday

• Ez 24:15-23 • (Ps) Dt 32:18-21 • Mt 19:16-22

_____

_____

_____

_____

_____

_____

_____

_____

_____

> The divine heart of our Savior is filled with eternal love for us.
> —**St. John Eudes**

SAINT JOHN EUDES
• Ez 28:1-10 • (Ps) Dt 32:26-28, 30, 35c-36b • Mt 19:23-30

19
Tuesday

_____

_____

_____

_____

_____

_____

_____

_____

_____

SAINT BERNARD
• Ez 34:1-11 • Ps 23:1-6 • Mt 20:1-16

20
Wednesday

_____

_____

_____

_____

_____

_____

_____

_____

_____

AUGUST

> The Blessed Virgin Mary should be called Queen . . .
> because God has willed her to have an exceptional role in the
> work of our eternal salvation.
>
> —Pope Pius XII

21
Thursday

SAINT PIUS X
• Ez 36:23-28 • Ps 51:12-15, 18-19 • Mt 22:1-14

_____
_____
_____
_____
_____
_____
_____
_____

22
Friday

THE QUEENSHIP OF THE BLESSED VIRGIN MARY
• Ez 37:1-14 • Ps 107:2-9 • Mt 22:34-40

_____
_____
_____
_____
_____
_____
_____
_____

When we serve the poor and the sick, we serve Jesus. We must not fail to help our neighbors, because in them we serve Jesus.

—St. Rose of Lima

Saint Rose of Lima
• Ez 43:1-7ab • Ps 85:9b-14 • Mt 23:1-12

23
Saturday

_____

_____

_____

_____

_____

_____

_____

_____

_____

_____

Twenty-first Sunday in Ordinary Time
• Is 22:19-23 • Ps 138:1-3, 6, 8 • Rom 11:33-36 • Mt 16:13-20

24
Sunday

_____

_____

_____

_____

_____

_____

_____

_____

_____

_____

AUGUST

In prosperity give thanks to God with humility and fear, lest by pride you abuse God's benefits and offend him.

—St. Louis of France

25
Monday

SAINT LOUIS; SAINT JOSEPH CALASANZ
• 2 Thes 1:1-5, 11-12 • Ps 96:1-5 • Mt 23:13-22

_____
_____
_____
_____
_____
_____
_____
_____
_____

26
Tuesday

• 2 Thes 2:1-3a, 14-17 • Ps 96:10-13 • Mt 23:23-26

_____
_____
_____
_____
_____
_____
_____
_____

Things are at rest when they are in their proper place. The proper place for the heart of a human being is the heart of God.

—St. Augustine

SAINT MONICA
• 2 Thes 3:6-10, 16-18 • Ps 128:1-2, 4-5 • Mt 23:27-32

27
Wednesday

_____

_____

_____

_____

_____

_____

_____

_____

_____

SAINT AUGUSTINE
• 1 Cor 1:1-9 • Ps 145:2-7 • Mt 24:42-51

28
Thursday

_____

_____

_____

_____

_____

_____

_____

_____

_____

_____

AUGUST

By celebrating [John the Baptist's] birth and martyrdom,
the Church unites herself to his desire:
He must increase, but I must decrease.

—*Catechism of the Catholic Church,* 524

29
Friday

THE PASSION OF SAINT JOHN THE BAPTIST
• 1 Cor 1:17-25 • Ps 33:1-2, 4-5, 10-11 • Mk 6:17-29

_____

_____

_____

_____

_____

_____

_____

_____

_____

30
Saturday

• 1 Cor 1:26-31 • Ps 33:12-13, 18-21 • Mt 25:14-30

_____

_____

_____

_____

_____

_____

_____

_____

_____

Intense love does not measure, . . . it just gives.
—Blessed Teresa of Calcutta

Twenty-second Sunday in Ordinary Time
• Jer 20:7-9 • Ps 63:2-6, 8-9 • Rom 12:1-2 • Mt 16:21-27

31
Sunday

_____

_____

_____

_____

_____

_____

_____

_____

_____

_____

_____

_____

_____

_____

_____

_____

_____

_____

_____

_____

_____

AUGUST

SEPTEMBER

My God, how great you are, how wonderful in all your works! Teach me your will that I may begin and end all my actions for your greater glory. . . . O my God, I thank you for the love that you have planted in my heart. I will cultivate this precious flower. I will guard it night and day that nothing may injure it. O Lord, water it with the dew of your grace. Amen.

—*St. John Neumann*

The Lord is good to all,
and his compassion is over all that he has made.

—**Psalm 145:9**

1
Monday

Labor Day (USA)
• 1 Cor 2:1-5 • Ps 119:97-102 • Lk 4:16-30

_____

_____

_____

_____

_____

_____

_____

_____

_____

2
Tuesday

• 1 Cor 2:10b-16 • Ps 145:8-14 • Lk 4:31-37

_____

_____

_____

_____

_____

_____

_____

_____

_____

Meditate daily on the words of your Creator. Learn the heart
of God in the words of God, that your soul may be enkindled
with greater longing for heavenly joys.

—**St. Gregory the Great**

SAINT GREGORY THE GREAT
• 1 Cor 3:1-9 • Ps 33:12-15, 20-21 • Lk 4:38-44

3
Wednesday

_____

_____

_____

_____

_____

_____

_____

_____

_____

• 1 Cor 3:18-23 • Ps 24:1b-6 • Lk 5:1-11

4
Thursday

_____

_____

_____

_____

_____

_____

_____

_____

_____

_____

SEPTEMBER

Commit your way to the LORD;
trust in him, and he will act.

—Psalm 37:5

5
Friday

• 1 Cor 4:1-5 • Ps 37:3-6, 27-28, 39-40 • Lk 5:33-39

_____

_____

_____

_____

_____

_____

_____

_____

6
Saturday

• 1 Cor 4:6b-15 • Ps 145:17-21 • Lk 6:1-5

_____

_____

_____

_____

_____

_____

_____

_____

_____

We [should] be filled with joy at the birth of Mary. Her womb was a most holy temple. There God received his human nature, and thus entered visibly into the world of men.

—St. Peter Damian

Twenty-third Sunday in Ordinary Time
• Ez 33:7-9 • Ps 95:1-2, 6-9 • Rom 13:8-10 • Mt 18:15-20

7
Sunday

_____
_____
_____
_____
_____
_____
_____
_____
_____

The Nativity of the Blessed Virgin Mary
• Mi 5:1-4a or Rom 8:28-30 • Ps 13:6 • Mt 1:1-16, 18-23

8
Monday

_____
_____
_____
_____
_____
_____
_____
_____
_____

SEPTEMBER

Seek God and endeavor to find him in all things.

—St. Peter Claver

9
Tuesday

SAINT PETER CLAVER
• 1 Cor 6:1-11 • Ps 149:1b-6a, 9b • Lk 6:12-19

_____

_____

_____

_____

_____

_____

_____

_____

_____

10
Wednesday

• 1 Cor 7:25-31 • Ps 45:11-12, 14-17 • Lk 6:20-26

_____

_____

_____

_____

_____

_____

_____

_____

_____

In doubts, in difficulties, call upon Mary. Don't let her name depart from your lips; never allow it to leave your heart.

—St. Bernard of Clairvaux

• 1 Cor 8:1b-7, 11-13 • Ps 139:1b-3, 13-14b, 23-24 • Lk 6:27-38

11
Thursday

_____
_____
_____
_____
_____
_____
_____
_____
_____
_____

THE MOST HOLY NAME OF MARY
• 1 Cor 9:16-19, 22b-27 • Ps 84:3-6, 12 • Lk 6:39-42

12
Friday

_____
_____
_____
_____
_____
_____
_____
_____
_____
_____

SEPTEMBER

The glory of the cross . . . has enlightened all those who were blinded by ignorance. It has set free all those who were slaves of sin. It has redeemed the whole human race.

—St. Cyril of Jerusalem

13
Saturday

SAINT JOHN CHRYSOSTOM
• 1 Cor 10:14-22 • Ps 116:12-13, 17-18 • Lk 6:43-49

_____

_____

_____

_____

_____

_____

_____

_____

_____

14
Sunday

THE EXALTATION OF THE HOLY CROSS
• Nm 21:4b-9 • Ps 78:1b-2, 34-38 • Phil 2:6-11 • Jn 3:13-17

_____

_____

_____

_____

_____

_____

_____

_____

_____

Only a consistency that lasts throughout the whole of life can be called faithfulness. Mary's *fiat* in the Annunciation finds its fullness in the silent *fiat* that she repeats at the foot of the cross.

—Blessed John Paul II

OUR LADY OF SORROWS
• 1 Cor 11:17-26, 33 • Ps 40:7-10, 17 • Jn 19:25-27 or Lk 2:33-35

15
Monday

_____

_____

_____

_____

_____

_____

_____

_____

_____

SAINTS CORNELIUS AND CYPRIAN
• 1 Cor 12:12-14, 27-31a • Ps 100:1b-5 • Lk 7:11-17

16
Tuesday

_____

_____

_____

_____

_____

_____

_____

_____

_____

SEPTEMBER

It is . . . necessary for us to get into the way of always and
instinctively turning to God.

—St. Robert Bellarmine

17
Wednesday

SAINT ROBERT BELLARMINE
• 1 Cor 12:31–13:13 • Ps 33:2-5, 12, 22 • Lk 7:31-35

_____
_____
_____
_____
_____
_____
_____
_____
_____

18
Thursday

• 1 Cor 15:1-11 • Ps 118:1b-2, 16-17, 28 • Lk 7:36-50

_____
_____
_____
_____
_____
_____
_____
_____
_____

Remain steadfast in faith, so that at last we will all
reach heaven and there rejoice together.

—St. Andrew Kim Taegon

SAINT JANUARIUS
• 1 Cor 15:12-20 • Ps 17:1, 6-8, 15 • Lk 8:1-3

19
Friday

_____

_____

_____

_____

_____

_____

_____

_____

_____

SAINTS ANDREW KIM TAE-GON AND
PAUL CHONG HA-SANG AND COMPANIONS
• 1 Cor 15:35-37, 42-49 • Ps 56:10c-14 • Lk 8:4-15

20
Saturday

_____

_____

_____

_____

_____

_____

_____

_____

_____

SEPTEMBER

Live your life in a manner worthy of the gospel of Christ.
—Philippians 1:27

21
Sunday

TWENTY-FIFTH SUNDAY IN ORDINARY TIME
• Is 55:6-9 • Ps 145:2-3, 8-9, 17-18 • Phil 1:20c-24, 27a • Mt 20:1-16a

_____
_____
_____
_____
_____
_____
_____
_____
_____

22
Monday

• Prv 3:27-34 • Ps 15:2-5 • Lk 8:16-18

_____
_____
_____
_____
_____
_____
_____
_____
_____

> If the soul longs for nothing else than to love its God,
> then don't worry and be quite sure that this soul possesses
> everything, that it possesses God himself.
>
> —St. Pio of Pietrelcina

SAINT PIO OF PIETRELCINA
• Prv 21:1-6, 10-13 • Ps 119:1, 27, 30, 34-35, 44 • Lk 8:19-21

23
Tuesday

_____

_____

_____

_____

_____

_____

_____

_____

_____

• Prv 30:5-9 • Ps 119:29, 72, 89, 101, 104, 163 • Lk 9:1-6

24
Wednesday

_____

_____

_____

_____

_____

_____

_____

_____

_____

_____

SEPTEMBER

Satisfy us in the morning with your steadfast love,
so that we may rejoice and be glad all our days.

—**Psalm 90:14**

25
Thursday

• Eccl 1:2-11 • Ps 90:3-6, 12-14, 17bc • Lk 9:7-9

_____

_____

_____

_____

_____

_____

_____

_____

_____

26
Friday

SAINTS COSMAS AND DAMIAN
• Eccl 3:1-11 • Ps 144:1b-4 • Lk 9:18-22

_____

_____

_____

_____

_____

_____

_____

_____

_____

> We should have no other object but God in our actions
> and seek to please him alone in all things.
>
> —St. Vincent de Paul

SAINT VINCENT DE PAUL
• Eccl 11:9–12:8 • Ps 90:3-6, 12-14, 17 • Lk 9:43b-45

27
Saturday

_____
_____
_____
_____
_____
_____
_____
_____
_____
_____

TWENTY-SIXTH SUNDAY IN ORDINARY TIME
• Ez 18:25-28 • Ps 25:4-5, 8-10, 14 • Phil 2:1-11 • Mt 21:28-32

28
Sunday

_____
_____
_____
_____
_____
_____
_____
_____
_____
_____

SEPTEMBER

The angels, wherever they may be sent, never stop gazing upon God. In the same way, a virtuous person, as much as he can, always keeps the memory of God in his heart.

—**St. Bonaventure**

29
Monday

SAINTS MICHAEL, GABRIEL, AND RAPHAEL, ARCHANGELS
• Dn 7:9-10, 13-14 or Rv 12:7-12a • Ps 138:1-5 • Jn 1:47-51

_____
_____
_____
_____
_____
_____
_____
_____
_____

30
Tuesday

SAINT JEROME
• Jb 3:1-3, 11-17, 20-23 • Ps 88:2-8 • Lk 9:51-56

_____
_____
_____
_____
_____
_____
_____
_____
_____

It is our part to seek, his to grant what we ask; ours to make a beginning, his to bring it to completion; ours to offer what we can, his to finish what we cannot.

—St. Jerome

_____

_____

_____

_____

_____

_____

_____

_____

_____

_____

_____

_____

_____

_____

_____

_____

_____

_____

_____

_____

_____

_____

_____

_____

_____

_____

_____

SEPTEMBER

OCTOBER

Lord, make us instruments of your peace.
Where there is hatred, let us sow love;
where there is injury, pardon;
where there is discord, union;
where there is doubt, faith;
where there is despair, hope;
where there is darkness, light;
where there is sadness, joy.

Grant that we may not so much seek
to be consoled as to console;
to be understood as to understand;
to be loved as to love.
For it is in giving that we receive;
it is in pardoning that we are pardoned;
and it is in dying that we are born to eternal life.
Amen.

—*St. Francis of Assisi*

Beside each believer stands an angel as protector
and shepherd, leading him to life.

—St. Basil the Great

1
Wednesday

SAINT THÉRÈSE OF THE CHILD JESUS
• Jb 9:1-12, 14-16 • Ps 88:10b-15 • Lk 9:57-62

_____

_____

_____

_____

_____

_____

_____

_____

_____

2
Thursday

THE HOLY GUARDIAN ANGELS
• Jb 19:21-27 • Ps 27:7-9, 13-14 • Mt 18:1-5, 10

_____

_____

_____

_____

_____

_____

_____

_____

_____

Almighty, most holy, most high and supreme God, highest good, all good, wholly good, who alone are good: To you we render all praise, all glory, all thanks, all honor, all blessing.

—**St. Francis of Assisi**

• Jb 38:1, 12-21; 40:3-5 • Ps 139:1-3, 7-10, 13-14b • Lk 10:13-16

3
Friday

_____
_____
_____
_____
_____
_____
_____
_____
_____
_____

SAINT FRANCIS OF ASSISI
• Jb 42:1-3, 5-6, 12-17 • Ps 119:66, 71, 75, 91, 125, 130 • Lk 10:17-24

4
Saturday

_____
_____
_____
_____
_____
_____
_____
_____
_____
_____

O CTOBER

Love God above all, so that warmed by his embrace,
you may be aflame with divine love.

—**St. Bruno**

5
Sunday

TWENTY-SEVENTH SUNDAY IN ORDINARY TIME
• Is 5:1-7 • Ps 80:9, 12-16, 19-20 • Phil 4:6-9 • Mt 21:33-43

_____

_____

_____

_____

_____

_____

_____

_____

_____

6
Monday

SAINT BRUNO; BLESSED MARIE ROSE DUROCHER
• Gal 1:6-12 • Ps 111:1b-2, 7-10 • Lk 10:25-37

_____

_____

_____

_____

_____

_____

_____

_____

With the Rosary, the Christian people sits at the school of Mary and is led to contemplate the beauty on the face of Christ and to experience the depths of his love.

—Blessed John Paul II

OUR LADY OF THE ROSARY
• Gal 1:13-24 • Ps 139:1b-3, 13-15 • Lk 10:38-42

7
Tuesday

• Gal 2:1-2, 7-14 • Ps 117:1b-2 • Lk 11:1-4

8
Wednesday

OCTOBER

Christ first of all.
                                        —St. John Leonardi

9
Thursday

SAINT DENIS AND COMPANIONS;
SAINT JOHN LEONARDI
• Gal 3:1-5 • (Ps) Lk 1:69-75 • Lk 11:5-13

_____
_____
_____
_____
_____
_____
_____
_____

10
Friday

• Gal 3:7-14 • Ps 111:1b-6 • Lk 11:15-26

_____
_____
_____
_____
_____
_____
_____
_____

My God will fully satisfy every need of yours according
to his riches in glory in Christ Jesus. To our God and Father
be glory forever and ever. Amen.

—Philippians 4:19-20

• Gal 3:22-29 • Ps 105:2-7 • Lk 11:27-28

11
Saturday

_____

_____

_____

_____

_____

_____

_____

_____

_____

Twenty-eighth Sunday in Ordinary Time
• Is 25:6-10a • Ps 23:1-6 • Phil 4:12-14, 19-20 • Mt 22:1-14

12
Sunday

_____

_____

_____

_____

_____

_____

_____

_____

_____

_____

OCTOBER

Let your steadfast love come to me, O LORD,
your salvation according to your promise.

—Psalm 119:41

13
Monday

• Gal 4:22-24, 26-27, 31–5:1 • Ps 113:1b-7 • Lk 11:29-32

_____

_____

_____

_____

_____

_____

_____

_____

_____

14
Tuesday

SAINT CALLISTUS I
• Gal 5:1-6 • Ps 119:41, 43-45, 47-48 • Lk 11:37-41

_____

_____

_____

_____

_____

_____

_____

_____

Our Lord Jesus Christ desires that we should . . .
glorify his all-loving Heart; for it was his Heart that suffered
the most in his sacred humanity.

—**St. Margaret Mary Alacoque**

SAINT TERESA OF JESUS
• Gal 5:18-25 • Ps 1:1-4, 6 • Lk 11:42-46

15
Wednesday

_____

_____

_____

_____

_____

_____

_____

_____

_____

SAINT HEDWIG; SAINT MARGARET MARY ALACOQUE
• Eph 1:1-10 • Ps 98:1-6 • Lk 11:47-54

16
Thursday

_____

_____

_____

_____

_____

_____

_____

_____

_____

_____

OCTOBER

He who died in place of us is the one object of my quest.
He who rose for our sakes is my one desire.

—**St. Ignatius of Antioch**

17
Friday

SAINT IGNATIUS OF ANTIOCH
• Eph 1:11-14 • Ps 33:1-2, 4-5, 12-13 • Lk 12:1-7

_____

_____

_____

_____

_____

_____

_____

_____

_____

18
Saturday

SAINT LUKE, EVANGELIST
• 2 Tm 4:10-17b • Ps 145:10-13, 17-18 • Lk 10:1-9

_____

_____

_____

_____

_____

_____

_____

_____

_____

Entrust yourself entirely to God. He is a Father,
and a most loving Father at that.

—St. Paul of the Cross

Twenty-ninth Sunday in Ordinary Time
• Is 45:1, 4-6 • Ps 96:1, 3-5, 7-10 • 1 Thes 1:1-5b • Mt 22:15-21

19
Sunday

_____

_____

_____

_____

_____

_____

_____

_____

_____

Saint Paul of the Cross
• Eph 2:1-10 • Ps 100:1b-5 • Lk 12:13-21

20
Monday

_____

_____

_____

_____

_____

_____

_____

_____

_____

OCTOBER

Surely God is my salvation;
I will trust, and will not be afraid.

—Isaiah 12:2

21
Tuesday

• Eph 2:12-22 • Ps 85:9-14 • Lk 12:35-38

_____
_____
_____
_____
_____
_____
_____
_____
_____

22
Wednesday

• Eph 3:2-12 • (Ps) Is 12:2-6 • Lk 12:39-48

_____
_____
_____
_____
_____
_____
_____
_____
_____

Those who are called to the table of the Lord must glow
with the brightness that comes from the good example of
a praiseworthy and blameless life.

—St. John of Capistrano

SAINT JOHN OF CAPISTRANO
• Eph 3:14-21 • Ps 33:1-2, 4-5, 11-12, 18-19 • Lk 12:49-53

23
Thursday

_____

_____

_____

_____

_____

_____

_____

_____

_____

_____

SAINT ANTHONY MARY CLARET
• Eph 4:1-6 • Ps 24:1-6 • Lk 12:54-59

24
Friday

_____

_____

_____

_____

_____

_____

_____

_____

_____

_____

OCTOBER

I love you, O LORD, my strength.
The LORD is my rock, my fortress, and my deliver,
my God, my rock in whom I take refuge.

—Psalm 18:1-2

25
Saturday

• Eph 4:7-16 • Ps 122:1-5 • Lk 13:1-9

_____
_____
_____
_____
_____
_____
_____
_____
_____

26
Sunday

THIRTIETH SUNDAY IN ORDINARY TIME
• Ex 22:20-26 • Ps 18:2-4, 47, 51 • 1 Thes 1:5c-10 • Mt 22:34-40

_____
_____
_____
_____
_____
_____
_____
_____
_____

Build yourselves up on your most holy faith, pray in the Holy Spirit; keep yourselves in the love of God, wait for the mercy of our Lord Jesus Christ unto eternal life.

—Jude 20-21

• Eph 4:32–5:8 • Ps 1:1-4, 6 • Lk 13:10-17

27
Monday

_____
_____
_____
_____
_____
_____
_____
_____
_____
_____

SAINTS SIMON AND JUDE, APOSTLES
• Eph 2:19-22 • Ps 19:2-5 • Lk 6:12-16

28
Tuesday

_____
_____
_____
_____
_____
_____
_____
_____
_____
_____

OCTOBER

Be strong in the Lord and in the strength of his power.
Put on the whole armor of God, so that you may be able to
stand against the wiles of the devil.

—**Ephesians 6:10-11**

29
Wednesday

• Eph 6:1-9 • Ps 145:10-14 • Lk 13:22-30

_____

_____

_____

_____

_____

_____

_____

_____

_____

30
Thursday

• Eph 6:10-20 • Ps 144:1-2, 9-10 • Lk 13:31-35

_____

_____

_____

_____

_____

_____

_____

_____

_____

The Catholic Church is not an archaeological museum.
It is the ancient village fountain that gives water to the
generations of today, as it gave it to those of days gone by.

—**Blessed John XXIII**

• Phil 1:1-11 • Ps 111:1-6 • Lk 14:1-6

31
Friday

O CTOBER

November

Ogive thanks to the Lord, call on his name,
   make known his deeds among the peoples.
Sing to him, sing praises to him,
   tell of all his wonderful works.
Glory in his holy name;
   let the hearts of those who seek the
      Lord rejoice!

—1 Chronicles 16:8-10

When we commemorate the saints, we are inflamed with another yearning: that Christ our life may also appear to us as he appeared to them and that we may one day share in his glory.

—St. Bernard of Clairvaux

1
Saturday

ALL SAINTS
• Rv 7:2-4, 9-14 • Ps 24:1b-6 • 1 Jn 3:1-3 • Mt 5:1-12a
Not a Holy Day of Obligation This Year

_____

_____

_____

_____

_____

_____

_____

_____

2
Sunday

THE COMMEMORATION OF ALL THE FAITHFUL
DEPARTED (ALL SOULS' DAY)
• Wis 3:1-9 • Ps 23:1-6 • Rom 5:5-11 or 6:3-9 • Jn 6:37-40

_____

_____

_____

_____

_____

_____

_____

_____

_____

May my soul never cease to praise the Lord,
who never ceases to lavish gifts.

—St. Charles Borromeo

SAINT MARTIN DE PORRES
• Phil 2:1-4 • Ps 131:1b-3 • Lk 14:12-14

3
Monday

_____

_____

_____

_____

_____

_____

_____

_____

_____

SAINT CHARLES BORROMEO
• Phil 2:5-11 • Ps 22:26b-32 • Lk 14:15-24

4
Tuesday

_____

_____

_____

_____

_____

_____

_____

_____

_____

NOVEMBER

> There will be more joy in heaven over one sinner
> who repents than over ninety-nine righteous persons
> who need no repentance.
>
> —Jesus in Luke 15:7

5
Wednesday

• Phil 2:12-18 • Ps 27:1, 4, 13-14 • Lk 14:25-33

_____
_____
_____
_____
_____
_____
_____
_____
_____

6
Thursday

• Phil 3:3-8a • Ps 105:2-7 • Lk 15:1-10

_____
_____
_____
_____
_____
_____
_____
_____
_____

Praise the LORD!
Happy are those who fear the LORD,
who greatly delight in his commandments.

—Psalm 112:1

• Phil 3:17–4:1 • Ps 122:1-5 • Lk 16:1-8

7
Friday

_____

_____

_____

_____

_____

_____

_____

_____

_____

_____

• Phil 4:10-19 • Ps 112:1b-2, 5-6, 8-9 • Lk 16:9-15

8
Saturday

_____

_____

_____

_____

_____

_____

_____

_____

_____

_____

NOVEMBER

No one should be ashamed of the cross of Christ,
through which the world has been redeemed.

—St. Leo the Great

9
Sunday

THE DEDICATION OF THE LATERAN BASILICA
• Ez 47:1-2, 8-9, 12 • Ps 46:2-3, 5-6, 8-9 • 1 Cor 3:9c-11, 16-17
• Jn 2:13-22

_____

_____

_____

_____

_____

_____

_____

_____

_____

10
Monday

SAINT LEO THE GREAT
• Ti 1:1-9 • Ps 24:1b-6 • Lk 17:1-6

_____

_____

_____

_____

_____

_____

_____

_____

_____

Martin of Tours, the soldier who became a monk and a bishop,
. . . is almost like an icon, illustrating the irreplaceable value of
the individual testimony to charity.

—**Pope Benedict XVI**

SAINT MARTIN OF TOURS
• Ti 2:1-8, 11-14 • Ps 37:3-4, 18, 23, 27, 29 • Lk 17:7-10

11
Tuesday

SAINT JOSAPHAT
• Ti 3:1-7 • Ps 23:1b-6 • Lk 17:11-19

12
Wednesday

NOVEMBER

> Lean on your Beloved, because the soul who abandons herself in the hands of Jesus in all she does is carried in his arms.
>
> —**St. Frances Xavier Cabrini**

13
Thursday

SAINT FRANCES XAVIER CABRINI
• Phlm 7-20 • Ps 146:7-10 • Lk 17:20-25

_____
_____
_____
_____
_____
_____
_____
_____
_____

14
Friday

• 2 Jn 4-9 • Ps 119:1-2, 10-11, 17-18 • Lk 17:26-37

_____
_____
_____
_____
_____
_____
_____
_____
_____

It is by the path of love, which is charity, that God draws
near to man, and man to God.

—St. Albert the Great

SAINT ALBERT THE GREAT
• 3 Jn 5-8 • Ps 112:1-6 • Lk 18:1-8

15
Saturday

_____
_____
_____
_____
_____
_____
_____
_____
_____
_____

THIRTY-THIRD SUNDAY IN ORDINARY TIME
• Prv 31:10-13, 19-20, 30-31 • Ps 128:1-5 • 1 Thes 5:1-6 • Mt 25:14-30

16
Sunday

_____
_____
_____
_____
_____
_____
_____
_____
_____
_____

NOVEMBER

As in heaven your will is punctually performed, so may it be done on earth by all creatures, particularly in me and by me.

—St. Elizabeth of Hungary

17
Monday

SAINT ELIZABETH OF HUNGARY
• Rv 1:1-4; 2:1-5 • Ps 1:1-4, 6 • Lk 18:35-43

_____
_____
_____
_____
_____
_____
_____
_____
_____

18
Tuesday

THE DEDICATION OF THE BASILICAS OF SAINTS PETER
AND PAUL; SAINT ROSE PHILIPPINE DUCHESNE
• Rv 3:1-6, 14-22 • Ps 15:2-5 • Lk 19:1-10 (or for the memorial of the
Dedication: • Acts 28:11-16, 30-31 • Ps 98:1-6 • Mt 14:22-33)

_____
_____
_____
_____
_____
_____
_____
_____
_____

Let everything that breathes praise the LORD!

—Psalm 150:6

• Rv 4:1-11 • Ps 150:1b-6 • Lk 19:11-28

19
Wednesday

_____
_____
_____
_____
_____
_____
_____
_____
_____
_____

• Rv 5:1-10 • Ps 149:1b-6a, 9b • Lk 19:41-44

20
Thursday

_____
_____
_____
_____
_____
_____
_____
_____
_____
_____
_____

NOVEMBER

> To die for Christ is not to sacrifice one's youth, but to renew it. Jesus Christ returns a hundredfold for all offered him, and adds to it eternal life.
>
> —**St. Cecilia**

21 Friday

THE PRESENTATION OF THE BLESSED VIRGIN MARY
• Rv 10:8-11 • Ps 119:14, 24, 72, 103, 111, 131 • Lk 19:45-48

_____

_____

_____

_____

_____

_____

_____

_____

22 Saturday

SAINT CECILIA
• Rv 11:4-12 • Ps 144:1-2, 9-10 • Lk 20:27-40

_____

_____

_____

_____

_____

_____

_____

_____

The throne of this King whom we worship . . . is the cross, and his triumph is the victory of Love, an almighty love that from the cross pours out his gifts upon humanity of all times and all places. —**Pope Benedict XVI**

OUR LORD JESUS CHRIST, KING OF THE UNIVERSE
• Ez 34:11-12, 15-17 • Ps 23:1-6 • 1 Cor 15:20-26, 28 • Mt 25:31-46

23
Sunday

_____

_____

_____

_____

_____

_____

_____

_____

_____

_____

SAINT ANDREW DUNG-LAC AND COMPANIONS
• Rv 14:1-3, 4b-5 • Ps 24:1b-6 • Lk 21:1-4

24
Monday

_____

_____

_____

_____

_____

_____

_____

_____

_____

_____

NOVEMBER

O sing to the LORD a new song,
for he has done marvelous things.

—Psalm 98:1

25 Tuesday

SAINT CATHERINE OF ALEXANDRIA
• Rv 14:14-19 • Ps 96:10-13 • Lk 21:5-11

_____
_____
_____
_____
_____
_____
_____
_____
_____

26 Wednesday

• Rv 15:1-4 • Ps 98:1-3b, 7-9 • Lk 21:12-19

_____
_____
_____
_____
_____
_____
_____
_____
_____

> Get used to lifting up your heart to God in acts of
> thanksgiving many times a day.
> — **St. Josemaría Escrivá**

THANKSGIVING DAY (USA)
• Rv 18:1-2, 21-23; 19:1-3, 9a • Ps 100:1b-5 • Lk 21:20-28

27
Thursday

_____

_____

_____

_____

_____

_____

_____

_____

_____

• Rv 20:1-4, 11–21:2 • Ps 84:3-6a, 8a • Lk 21:29-33

28
Friday

_____

_____

_____

_____

_____

_____

_____

_____

_____

NOVEMBER

We should always observe Advent with faith and love,
offering praise and thanksgiving to the Father for the mercy
and love he has shown us in this mystery.

—**St. Charles Borromeo**

29
Saturday

• Rv 22:1-7 • Ps 95:1-7b • Lk 21:34-36

_____

_____

_____

_____

_____

_____

_____

_____

30
Sunday

FIRST SUNDAY OF ADVENT
• Is 63:16b-17, 19b; 64:2-7 • Ps 80:2-3, 15-16, 18-19
• 1 Cor 1:3-9 • Mk 13:33-37

_____

_____

_____

_____

_____

_____

_____

_____

Steep yourself in the meaning of these Advent days, and above all, pay heed to him who is approaching; . . . consider his purpose in coming, the ripeness of the times, the route he may choose for his approach. —St. Bernard of Clairvaux

N OVEMBER

DECEMBER

Keep us alert, we pray, O Lord our God,
as we await the advent of Christ your Son,
so that, when he comes and knocks,
he may find us watchful in prayer
and exultant in his praise.
Who lives and reigns with you in the unity
    of the Holy Spirit,
one God, for ever and ever.

—*Collect, Monday of the First Week of Advent*

Every year Advent reminds us that grace—and that is God's will
to save man—is more powerful than sin.

—**Blessed John Paul II**

1
Monday

• Is 2:1-5 • Ps 122:1-9 • Mt 8:5-11

_____
_____
_____
_____
_____
_____
_____
_____
_____

2
Tuesday

• Is 11:1-10 • Ps 72:1-2, 7-8, 12-13, 17 • Lk 10:21-24

_____
_____
_____
_____
_____
_____
_____
_____
_____

God our Lord knows the intentions which he in his mercy has wished to place in us, and the great hope and confidence which he in his goodness has wished that we should have in him.

—St. Francis Xavier

SAINT FRANCIS XAVIER

• Is 25:6-10a • Ps 23:1-6 • Mt 15:29-37

3
Wednesday

_____

_____

_____

_____

_____

_____

_____

_____

_____

_____

SAINT JOHN DAMASCENE

• Is 26:1-6 • Ps 118:1, 8-9, 19-21, 25-27a • Mt 7:21, 24-27

4
Thursday

_____

_____

_____

_____

_____

_____

_____

_____

_____

_____

DECEMBER

As the season for commemorating [Christ's] birth approaches, something stirs in us, something deep and profound, as if we are expecting a great miracle.

—**Catherine Doherty**

5
Friday

• Is 29:17-24 • Ps 27:1, 4, 13-14 • Mt 9:27-31

_____
_____
_____
_____
_____
_____
_____
_____
_____

6
Saturday

SAINT NICHOLAS
• Is 30:19-21, 23-26 • Ps 147:1-6 • Mt 9:35–10:1, 5a, 6-8

_____
_____
_____
_____
_____
_____
_____
_____
_____

In Mary Immaculate we contemplate the reflection
of the Beauty that saves the world: the beauty of God
that shines on the face of Christ.

—Pope Benedict XVI

SECOND SUNDAY OF ADVENT

• Is 40:1-5, 9-11 • Ps 85:9-14 • 2 Pt 3:8-14 • Mk 1:1-8

7
Sunday

_____

_____

_____

_____

_____

_____

_____

_____

_____

_____

THE IMMACULATE CONCEPTION OF THE
BLESSED VIRGIN MARY

• Gn 3:9-15, 20 • Ps 98:1-4 • Eph 1:3-6, 11-12 • Lk 1:26-38
Holy Day of Obligation

8
Monday

_____

_____

_____

_____

_____

_____

_____

_____

_____

DECEMBER

> I am a compassionate mother to you and to all of my devoted children who will call upon me with confidence.
>
> —**Our Lady to St. Juan Diego**

9
Tuesday

SAINT JUAN DIEGO
• Is 40:1-11 • Ps 96:1-3, 10-13 • Mt 18:12-14

_____
_____
_____
_____
_____
_____
_____
_____
_____

10
Wednesday

• Is 40:25-31 • Ps 103:1-4, 8, 10 • Mt 11:28-30

_____
_____
_____
_____
_____
_____
_____
_____

Our Lady of Guadalupe continues to be a great sign of Christ's nearness to us today. She extends an invitation to all men and women to enter into communion with the Father.

—**Blessed John Paul II**

SAINT DAMASUS I
• Is 41:13-20 • Ps 145:1, 9-13b • Mt 11:11-15

11
Thursday

_____
_____
_____
_____
_____
_____
_____
_____
_____
_____

OUR LADY OF GUADALUPE
• Zec 2:14-17 or Rv 11:19a; 12:1-6a, 10ab • (Ps) Jdt 13:18b-19
• Lk 1:26-38 or Lk 1:39-47

12
Friday

_____
_____
_____
_____
_____
_____
_____
_____
_____
_____

DECEMBER

> The virgin comes walking, / the Word in her womb. / Could you
> not give her / a place in your room?
>
> —St. John of the Cross

13
Saturday

SAINT LUCY
• Sir 48:1-4, 9-11 • Ps 80:2-3, 15-16, 18-19 • Mt 17:9a, 10-13

_____
_____
_____
_____
_____
_____
_____
_____
_____

14
Sunday

THIRD SUNDAY OF ADVENT
• Is 61:1-2a, 10-11 • (Ps) Lk 1:46-50, 53-54 • 1 Thes 5:16-24
• Jn 1:6-8, 19-28

_____
_____
_____
_____
_____
_____
_____
_____
_____

Advent is the season of the secret, the secret of the growth
of Christ, of Divine Love growing in silence.
—Caryll Houselander

• Nm 24:2-7, 15-17a • Ps 25:4-9 • Mt 21:23-27

15
Monday

_____
_____
_____
_____
_____
_____
_____
_____
_____
_____

• Zep 3:1-2, 9-13 • Ps 34:2-3, 6-7, 17-19, 23 • Mt 21:28-32

16
Tuesday

_____
_____
_____
_____
_____
_____
_____
_____
_____
_____

DECEMBER

The spirit of Advent largely consists in living close to Our Lady
during the time she is carrying Jesus in her womb.

—**Francis Fernandez**

17
Wednesday

• Gn 49:2, 8-10 • Ps 72:1-4b, 7-8, 17 • Mt 1:1-17

_____
_____
_____
_____
_____
_____
_____
_____

18
Thursday

• Jer 23:5-8 • Ps 72:1-2, 12-13, 18-19 • Mt 1:18-25

_____
_____
_____
_____
_____
_____
_____
_____
_____

The Lord himself will give you a sign. Look, the young woman is
with child and shall bear a son, and shall name him Immanuel

—**Isaiah 7:14**

• Jgs 13:2-7, 24-25a • Ps 71:3-6b, 16-17 • Lk 1:5-25

19
Friday

_____

_____

_____

_____

_____

_____

_____

_____

_____

• Is 7:10-14 • Ps 24:1-6 • Lk 1:26-38

20
Saturday

_____

_____

_____

_____

_____

_____

_____

_____

_____

_____

DECEMBER

The Virgin became pregnant with the Incarnation of Christ,
may our hearts become pregnant with faith in Christ;
she brought forth the Savior, may our souls bring forth
salvation and praise.

—St. Augustine

21
Sunday

FOURTH SUNDAY OF ADVENT
• 2 Sm 7:1-5, 8b-12, 14a, 16 • Ps 89:2-5, 27, 29 • Rom 16:25-27
• Lk 1:26-38

_____

_____

_____

_____

_____

_____

_____

_____

22
Monday

• 1 Sm 1:24-28 • (Ps) 1 Sm 2:1, 4-8 • Lk 1:46-56

_____

_____

_____

_____

_____

_____

_____

_____

_____

Arise, everyone! Mary invites us all—rich and poor, the just and sinners—to enter the cave of Bethlehem, to adore and to kiss the feet of her newborn Son. . . . Let us enter and not be afraid.

—**St. Alphonsus Liguori**

SAINT JOHN OF KANTY
• Mal 3:1-4, 23-24 • Ps 25:4-5b, 8-10, 14 • Lk 1:57-66

23
Tuesday

_____

_____

_____

_____

_____

_____

_____

_____

_____

_____

• 2 Sm 7:1-5, 8b-12, 14a, 16 • Ps 89:2-5, 27, 29 • Lk 1:67-79

24
Wednesday

_____

_____

_____

_____

_____

_____

_____

_____

_____

_____

DECEMBER

The Child, the Lord Jesus Christ . . . Word in our flesh,
Wisdom in infancy, Power in weakness, and in true Man,
the Lord of Majesty.

—St. Leo the Great

25
Thursday

THE NATIVITY OF THE LORD (CHRISTMAS)
• Is 52:7-10 • Ps 98:1-6 • Heb 1:1-6 • Jn 1:1-18
Holy Day of Obligation

_____

_____

_____

_____

_____

_____

_____

_____

_____

26
Friday

SAINT STEPHEN, THE FIRST MARTYR
• Acts 6:8-10; 7:54-59 • Ps 31:3c-4, 6, 8ab, 16b-17 • Mt 10:17-22

_____

_____

_____

_____

_____

_____

_____

_____

_____

_____

> May the Holy Family, icon and model of every human family,
> help each individual to walk in the spirit of Nazareth.
> —**Blessed John Paul II**

SAINT JOHN, APOSTLE AND EVANGELIST
• 1 Jn 1:1-4 • Ps 97:1-2, 5-6, 11-12 • Jn 20:1a, 2-8

27
Saturday

_____

_____

_____

_____

_____

_____

_____

_____

_____

_____

THE HOLY FAMILY OF JESUS, MARY, AND JOSEPH
• Sir 3:2-6, 12-14 or Gn 15:1-6; 21:1-3 • Ps 128:1-5 or Ps 105:1-6, 8-9
• Col 3:12-21 or Heb 11:8, 11-12, 17-19 • Lk 2:22-40

28
Sunday

_____

_____

_____

_____

_____

_____

_____

_____

_____

_____

DECEMBER

Christ . . . now looks down from heaven on our actions
and secret thoughts, and one day he will give each of us the
reward his deeds deserve.

—**St. Thomas Becket**

29
Monday

SAINT THOMAS BECKET
• 1 Jn 2:3-11 • Ps 96:1-3, 5b-6 • Lk 2:22-35

_____

_____

_____

_____

_____

_____

_____

_____

_____

30
Tuesday

• 1 Jn 2:12-17 • Ps 96:7-10 • Lk 2:36-40

_____

_____

_____

_____

_____

_____

_____

_____

_____

The object of a New Year is not that we should have a new year.
It is that we should have a new soul.

—G.K. Chesterton

SAINT SYLVESTER I
• 1 Jn 2:18-21 • Ps 96:1-2, 11-13 • Jn 1:1-18

31
Wednesday

_____

_____

_____

_____

_____

_____

_____

_____

_____

_____

_____

_____

_____

_____

_____

_____

_____

_____

_____

_____

_____

DECEMBER

Reserve Next Year's *Prayer Journal* Today!

The Word Among Us *2015 Prayer Journal*

Continue your journey of faith with next year's *Prayer Journal*. As always, you'll get inspirational quotes and a complete listing of the daily Mass readings, saints' feast days, and holy days of obligation. Give it as a gift and introduce a friend to the pleasures of journaling.

—Also Available—

Abide in My Word 2015: Mass Readings at Your Fingertips

Keep abreast with the daily Mass readings and make personal Scripture reading easier! *Abide in My Word* provides each day's Scripture readings in an easy-to-locate format. Each day is clearly listed so that it only takes a few minutes to draw near to the Lord through the Mass readings. Use it together with your *Prayer Journal*.

To order, use the card below or call **1-800-775-9673**

You'll find up-to-date product information on our Web site at www.wau.org

Fill in the card below and mail in an envelope to:

The Word Among Us
7115 Guilford Drive, Suite 100
Frederick, MD 21704

Order 2 or more copies and save 10%!

- [ ] **YES!** Send me _____ copies of the *2015 Prayer Journal*. JP2C
(1 @ $13.95; 2 or more @ $12.56 each plus shipping and handling)

- [ ] **YES!** Send me _____ copies of *Abide in My Word 2015*. AB2C
(1 *Abide in My Word* @ $16.50; 2 or more @ $14.85 each plus shipping and handling)

- [ ] **YES!** Send me the *2015 Prayer Journal* **AND** *2015 Abide in My Word* for only $27.60 plus shipping and handling! 15SE

Name _____

Address _____

City _____

State _____ Zip _____

Phone ( ) _____

E-mail (optional) _____

Send no money now. We will bill you.   VISA MasterCard NOVUS

SHIPPING & HANDLING (Add to total product order):					
If your subtotal is:	$0-15	$16-$35	$36-50	$51-75	$76-100
Add shipping of:	$5	$7	$9	$11	$13

CPPJ14Z